Literacy Activity Book

Year 3

Ray Barker and Louis Fidge

Letts
EDUCATIONAL

Every effort has been made to trace copyright holders and to obtain their permission for the use of copyright material. The authors and publishers would gladly receive information enabling them to rectify any error or omission in subsequent editions.

Acknowledgements
Josie Smith at the Seaside by Magdalen Nabb published by HarperCollins Publishers Ltd; *'Weather'* from First Rhymes by Lucy Coats (illustrated in the original publication by Selina Young), first published in the UK by Orchard Books, a division of the Watts Publishing Group, 96 Leonard Street, London EC2A 4RH; *Chips and Jessie* by Shirley Hughes, published by Bodley Head; *The Battle of Bubble and Squeak* by Phillipa Pearce, published by Scholastic Children's Books; *The Birthday Surprise* by Julia Donaldson, published by Ginn; the extract from *'Puppy and I'* from When We Were Very Young, published by Methuen Children's Books 1924 (a division of Reed International Books Ltd); the extract from *'Rap Connected'* from Talking Turkeys by Benjamin Zephaniah, published by Puffin Children's Books; *Indian Legends of the Pacific Northwest* by Ella Clark, published by the University of California, (1953 The Regents of the University of California, renewed 1981 Ella E. Clark; *On the Run* by Nina Bawden published by Hamish Hamilton; *Fantastic Mr Fox* by Roald Dahl, published by Cape; *The BFG* by Roald Dahl, published by Cape; *'The Adventures of Isabel'* (1936 by Ogden Nash, Renewed. reprinted by permission of Curtis Brown Ltd.

First published 1998

Letts Educational, Schools and Colleges Division,
9-15 Aldine Street, London W12 8AW
Tel: 0181 740 2270   Fax: 0181 740 2280

Text © Ray Barker and Louis Fidge

Designed edited and produced by Gecko Limited, Bicester, Oxon

Illustrations © Richard Adams (The Inkshed), Kiran Ahmad, Sally Artz, Jonathan Bentley (Beint & Beint), Liz Catchpole, John Eastwood (Maggie Mundy Illustration Agency), David Frankland (Artist Partners), Gecko Limited, Tania Hurt-Newton, Steve Lach, Doreen McGuiness, Robert McPhillips, Shelagh McNicholas, Dave Mostyn, Jan Nesbit, Andrew Warrington

British Library Cataloguing-in-Publication Data
A CIP record for this book is available from the British Library

ISBN 184085 0639

Printed in Great Britain by Clowes Group Ltd

Letts Educational is the trading name of BPP [Letts Educational] Ltd

Introduction

The Literacy Textbooks:

- support the teaching of the Literacy Hour
- help meet the majority of the objectives of the National Literacy Strategy Framework
- are divided into 3 sections, each sufficient for one term's work
- contain ten units per term, each equivalent to a week's work
- provide two Self Assessment units in each term to check on progress
- contain two Writing Focus units each term to support compositional writing
- include a Glossary of definitions of terms used in the book
- list High Frequency Words at the back of the Year 3, 4 and 5 textbooks
- provide coverage of a wide range of writing, both fiction and non-fiction as identified in the National Literacy Strategy Framework.

Unit number →
Text for reading and discussion
Key teaching points
Text Level activities (purple)
Sentence Level activities (yellow)
Word Level activities (green)

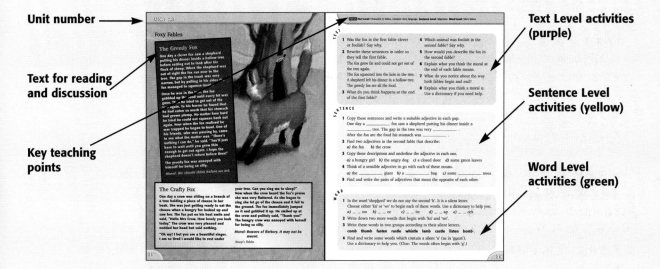

Self Assessment units:

- appear after every five units
- review the key objectives at Sentence Level and Word Level in the preceding five units
- contain a spelling chart to support the teaching of spelling strategies
- may be used to provide:
  - a review of progress when completed and kept as a record
  - further practice in areas of concern
  - homework assignments.

The Glossary:

- explains and gives examples of key words and concepts
- may be used for teaching purposes or for reference by the pupil.

Writing Focus units:

- appear after every five units of work
- develop work covered in the preceding five teaching units
- support work on compositional writing
- contain support for the teaching of different essential writing skills, e.g. how to plan a story.

High Frequency Word lists:

- contain words that occur frequently in children's reading and writing
- help children to recognise these words and to spell them correctly
- are often referred to and used in the activities in the book
- provide an easily accessible resource for spelling activities.

	Focus	
Text Level	**Sentence Level**	**Word Level**

<table>
<tr><td rowspan="2">Term 1</td><td>

- Story settings
- Shape poetry
- Poetry
- Story setting
- Settings and characters playscripts

</td><td>

Introducing dialogue
Verb tenses
Grammatical awareness; Punctuation
Presentation of text
General punctuation

</td><td>

Prefixes
Syllables
Phonemes; Spelling strategies
Proof reading for spelling mistakes
Phonemes; Spelling strategies

</td></tr>
<tr><td colspan="3">

Writing Focus 1.1   Story structure; Story settings; Shape poems; Plays; Handy hints for writing stories
Self Assessment 1.1   Review of Word and Sentence Level Units 1.1 – 1.5; Handy hints for spelling

</td></tr>
</table>

• Story setting	Speech marks	Words ending with 'le'
• Using a dictionary and thesaurus	Verbs	Synonyms; Alphabetical order
• Main points; Fiction; non-fiction	Verbs	Verbs ending in 'ing'
• Locating information	Commas in lists	Spelling strategies
• Playscripts	Types of sentences	Phonemes

Writing Focus 1.2   Labelling; Presenting information; Writing reports; Handy hints on checking your work
Self Assessment 1.2   Review of Word and Sentence Level Units 1.6 – 1.10; Handy hints for spelling

Term 2

• Story themes; Key incidents	Common nouns	Singular and plural
• Story themes; Characterisation	Common and collective nouns	Singular and plural
• Characterisation; Story language	Adjectives	Silent letters
• Characterisation	Adjectives	Suffixes
• Performance poetry	Use of 1st and 3rd person; Capitals	Suffixes; Apostrophes (Contractions)

Writing Focus 2.1   Story structure; Story sequels; Fairy stories/traditional tales; Handy hints for writing fairy stories
Self Assessment 2.1   Review of Word and Sentence Level Units 2.1 – 2.5; Handy hints for spelling

• Characterisation; Story themes	Use of commas	Compound words
• Performance poetry	Subject/verb agreement	Dictionary skills
• Features of non-fiction	Notes	Proof-reading for spelling errors
• Instructions	Punctuation; Correct sentences	Spelling strategies
• Characterisation; Story themes	Key words; Grammatical awareness	Syllables

Writing Focus 2.2   Giving instructions; Plans; Rules; Handy hints on editing your work
Self Assessment 2.2   Review of Word and Sentence Level Units 2.6 – 2.10; Handy hints for spelling

• Characterisation	Adjectives	Prefixes
• Fact and fiction; 'Time' words	Personal Pronouns – singular and plural	Words within words
• Stories by same author	Pronouns; Subject/verb agreement	Synonyms and homonyms
• Author language; Prediction	Use of 1st and 3rd person	Spelling strategies
• Fact and fiction	Conjunctions; Word order	Syllables

Writing Focus 3.1   Story sequel; Story plans; Writing stories; Making a book; Book reviews; Handy hints for writing stories
Self Assessment 3.1   Review of Word and Sentence Level Units 3.1 – 3.5; Handy hints for spelling

Term 3

• Humorous poetry	Sense and accuracy	Spelling strategies; Phonemes
• Types of letter; Audience	Possessive pronouns	Common expressions
• Locating facts; Alphabetic texts	Conjunctions; Past tenses	Apostrophes; Spelling
• Word puzzles, puns and riddles	Punctuation	Spelling strategies
• Library classification systems	Grammatical sense and accuracy	Spelling strategies

Writing Focus 3.2   Writing Letters; Make a non-fiction book; Handy hints on editing your work
Self Assessment 3.2   Review of Word and Sentence Level Units 3.6 – 3.10; Handy hints for spelling

CONTENTS

The Sandcastle

Josie Smith was on holiday at the seaside. She had spent all her money on a windmill for her sister, but what she really wanted was some flags for her own sandcastle.

"It's finished," called Josie Smith, and she was just going to say, "Can I have some flags for it?" when she remembered. She'd spent all her money on Eileen's windmill.

"What's the matter?" asked Josie's gran. "Are you wishing you still had your spending money?"

Josie Smith closed her eyes and tried to say, "No," but she couldn't. She closed her eyes tighter and some little tears squeezed out. She opened her eyes and looked up the sands and down the sands and saw everybody else's castles with red, white and blue flags on them.

"I don't want to dig any more," said Josie Smith, and her face felt hot and tired.

"If you're tired," said Josie's gran, "you can sit on my deck chair. I'm going for a little walk. And if you're careful with them, you can wear my sunglasses as well. Do you want to?"

"Yes," answered Josie Smith. And she sat in her gran's deck chair and looked through her gran's sunglasses that made the sea look brown and sad. Josie Smith didn't like the seaside so much any more. She wanted to go home.

"Here I am," said Josie's gran. "I'm really enjoying myself. I just wish I had a big sandcastle like yours but I'm too old to build one."

"You can have mine," said Josie Smith. "I don't like it any more."

"Well," replied Josie's gran, "that's very nice of you but I like a sandcastle with flags on it, myself."

"I haven't got any flags," said Josie Smith, and some more tears squeezed out and rolled down under her gran's sunglasses.

"You haven't got any flags?" said Josie's gran. "Well, a sandcastle's no good without flags. We'd better see if there are any in that magic handbag of mine."

From Josie Smith at the Seaside *by Magdalen Nabb*

T E X T

1 What is the title of the book from which this passage came?

2 What do the titles of the book and the passage tell you before you begin to read?

3 Before the passage begins there are some sentences written in *italics*.
   What do these sentences tell you?

4 What clues can you find in the passage that tell you it is about the seaside?
   Write them down, e.g. Gran was sitting on a deck chair, wearing sunglasses.

5 What other things at the seaside do you think Josie might:
   a) see   *b)* hear   *c)* smell?

6 What was the weather like? How do you know?

7 Who was Josie with at the seaside?

S E N T E N C E

1 This passage contains a lot of dialogue. How many times does the author use the word 'said' in the passage?

2 Find and write down some other words the author uses instead of 'said'.

3 Copy the conversation on the right. Choose a suitable word from this list to fill in each gap.

   replied sobbed called shouted suggested cried

"Look out! There's a big wave coming!"
_____ Gran.
"Help! It's splashed all over me!"_____ Josie Smith.
"Oh no! It's washed your sandcastle away,"_____ Gran.
"My lovely sandcastle is ruined!"
_____ Josie.
"Never mind. Let's go and have an ice cream,"_____ Gran.
"That's a good idea,"_____ Josie.

W O R D

1 Choose the prefix 'un' or 'dis' to go in front of each verb to give it the opposite meaning. Do it like this: pack – unpack
   a) do   *b)* appear   *c)* agree   *d)* tie   *e)* dress

2 Use a dictionary to find some more words beginning with 'un' or 'dis'.

3 Use a dictionary. Copy and complete each word below with one of the following prefixes: 'de' 're' 'pre'
   a) fill   *b)* scribe   *c)* pare   *d)* vent   *e)* turn   *f)* lay

4 Write five sentences using some of the words above in each one.

Shape Poems

LIGHTNING

1

LIGHTNING STREAKS,
LIGHTNING FLASHES,
LIGHTNING SIZZLES,
LIGHTNING
CRASHES

A SOFT HISSING SOUND...

HISS

SLITHERY SNAKES SLIDE ON THE GROUND, MAKING

3

ROAR

SPARK

BLAZE

HISS

4

2

MAKE A SNOWMAN
ROUND AND FAT,
ARROT FOR A NOSE,
BOBBLE HAT,
HANDS GET COLD,
STOP A WHILE...
TONES FOR BUTTONS,
STONY SMILE.

LEAP

SNAP

CRACKLE

ROGS

HOP AND

JUMP

5

8

TEXT

1 What do you notice about the poems and words opposite?
Why do you think the page is called 'Shape Poems'?

2 *a)* Write what each poem is about. Do it like this: Number 1 is about lightning.
b) Say how the shape or picture for each poem helps.

3 *a)* Copy 1 and underline the verbs like this: Lightning <u>flashes</u>.

b) Do the same for number 5.

4 The words used all describe the movements or sound of fireworks in number 4.
Write some words to describe the colour of fireworks.

5 Read number 3 again. What letter sound is used a lot? Why is this?

6 *a)* Which of the poems rhyme? *b)* Which of the rhyming poems do you like best?
Say why. *c)* Do all poems have to rhyme?

SENTENCE

1 Copy these sentences. Write in the correct form of the missing verb.

Do it like this: The snake hisses. Yesterday the snake hissed.

a) The hen clucks. Yesterday the hen _____ .
b) The duck quacks. Yesterday the duck _____ .
c) The bird sings. Yesterday the bird _____ .

4 I catch the ball. Yesterday I _____ the ball.

5 I see a cat. Yesterday I _____ two cats.

6 Tom goes to school. Yesterday he _____ to the shops.

WORD

1 Say these words slowly and listen to them: **lightning   mutter   snowman**
Can you hear their two parts (syllables)? Copy the words below. Say if they have
one or two syllables. Do it like this: *a)* the (1) *b)* snowman (2)
a) the   *b)* snowman   *c)* lightning   *d)* on   *e)* mutter   *f)* with   *g)* sliding
h) fat   *i)* button   *j)* and

2 Find and write 10 words with two syllables on the page opposite.

3 Use a dictionary to find the meaning of these words:

a) murmur   *b)* blaze   *c)* belching   *d)* leap   *e)* sizzle

4 Write a word that rhymes with:

a) round   *b)* fat   *c)* choke   *d)* slide   *e)* hop   *f)* scream

Weather

January new beginning,
Resolutions, snowflakes spinning.

February frosty fogs,
Winter shivers, fire-warm logs.

March blows windy, smells of spring,
Leaves peek out, brave blackbirds sing.

April showers fall soft and slow,
Earth wakes up, and green things grow.

May Day ribbons round a pole,
May-time babies, lamb and foal.

June brings summer blazing in,
Scent of roses, sun on skin.

July joy means school is out,
Time for picnics, heat and drought.

August goes on holiday,
Sandy castles, friends to stay.

September sees the autumn come,
Plough the fields, one by one.

October gales lash the trees,
Leaves a-swirling, crashing seas.

November nights all crisp and cold,
Winter coats for young and old.

December dark, yet full of light,
Christmas carols, stars so bright.

Lucy Coates

TEXT

1 Copy and complete these sentences:
   a) The poem is all about the
      w _ _ _ _ _ _ .
   b) Each verse is about a different
      m _ _ _ _ .

2 In which month does it say that
   a) it snows? *b)* there are showers?
   c) the autumn comes?
   d) the nights are crisp and cold?

3 What do you think these words mean:
   a) winter shivers   *b)* Earth wakes up
   c) gales lash the trees
   d) December dark, yet full of light

4 In the poem, find some things
   a) that are cold   *b)* that are hot
   c) that you smell   *d)* that you see
   e) that you hear

5 Find a word that rhymes with
   a) light   *b)* trees   *c)* spring
   d) fogs   *e)* out   *f)* old   *g)* pole

6 What did you think of the poem?
   Explain your answer.

7 Find and copy another poem about
   the weather. Which poem do you
   prefer? Why?

SENTENCE

Copy and complete these sentences
with a suitable word. Punctuate the
sentences correctly.

1 january is a cold _____
2 it often _____ in january
3 march comes _____ february
4 christmas is in _____
5 _____ comes before july
6 many people go on holiday in
   _____

7 is october after november
8 when does it rain most
9 january february march and april
   are the first four months of the year.

WORD

1 There are twelve words hiding in
   this puzzle. Find them and write
   them in your book.

o	t	h	e	r	a	f	b	u	r	n	g
b	c	g	i	r	l	d	e	s	t	i	r
h	w	e	r	e	j	t	u	r	n	k	m
h	u	r	t	n	q	m	e	m	b	e	r
s	t	b	i	r	d	u	t	e	r	m	v
t	h	i	r	s	t	w	x	f	u	r	a

2 Now write the words again in three
   sets according to the way they
   are spelt.

3 Choose two words from each set
   and write some sentences
   containing them.

Going Shopping

From Chips and Jessie
by Shirley Hughes

TEXT

1 Where does the story take place? How can you tell?

2 What is the name of:
   a) the boy   b) the baby
   c) the dog   d) the girl?

3 a) What is Chips' mum reading in the first picture?
   b) Why do you think she is doing this?
   c) What other things might she want to buy?

4 How can you tell the dog outside the supermarket is fed up?

5 Why are dogs not allowed in food shops?

6 What does Chips' mum tell him to do outside the supermarket?

7 Which things do you think Chips' mum asks him to get from the list?

SENTENCE

1 Is the page opposite from a story book or from an information book? Give a reason.

2 What is the main difference between the story opposite and the story in Unit 1.1?

3 Why does the writer use speech bubbles?

4 How is the bubble which comes from the dog different from the bubbles that come from Chips? Why do you think this is?

5 Find a word that is written in capital letters in the middle of a sentence. Copy the sentence and explain why you think the writer has written it this way.

6 Write down some of the other ways in which capital letters have been used, e.g. to begin sentences.

7 Draw a picture of Chips answering Jessie. Write down what you think he says in a speech bubble.

WORD

1 Copy the sentences below and use the words in the list to help you correct the spelling mistakes.

**looked shopping girl friend
told went saw tail some fast**

Chips and his mum and sister ~~whent~~ ~~shoping~~. Outside the supermarket they ~~sore~~ Jessie's dog. It ~~lookt~~ bored but when the dog saw Chips it wagged its ~~tayl~~. The dog was glad to see a ~~freind~~. In the shop, Chips' mum ~~toled~~ him to get ~~sum~~ things from the list. Chips pushed Gloria in a trolley. He ran ~~farst~~. Around one corner he met a ~~gurl~~ he knew.

2 Now write down each word from the list above. Think of at least one other word that contains the same letter pattern. Do it like this: went – bent, sent, dent.

Nail Soup

Narrator: Once upon a time there was a poor beggar. He had no money and was always hungry. One day as he was walking through a village he saw a nail on the ground. As he bent down to pick it up he had an idea.

Old lady: Good morning. What's that you've got there?

Man: It's a nail for making soup. If you let me come in I'll show you.

Narrator: So the old lady took the man into her house and gave him a pan and some water. The man put the nail into the pan and began to boil up the water. He took a deep sniff.

Man: This is going to be the best soup ever! Have you got such a thing as a carrot? It needs a bit of colour.

Narrator: The old lady gave him the carrot and he put it in the soup. The man stirred it and sniffed it again.

Man: Can I have an onion? That would help give it more flavour.

Narrator: The man chuckled slyly to himself.

Man: All it needs now is a chicken and some salt and pepper to finish it off.

Narrator: The old lady hurried off and got the things the beggar asked for. The smell was delicious. A little later the soup was ready to serve.

Man: Shall we have some nice, fresh, crispy, crusty bread to go with it?

Old lady: Of course. I'll just get some.

Narrator: When she returned they sat down and ate the soup.

Old lady: This is marvellous! I wish I had a nail like yours for making soup.

Man: They are not easy to come by, you know. But as you've been so kind to me, you can have mine as a special gift.

Narrator: The old lady held the nail tightly as she waved goodbye to the man. The man whistled happily to himself and smiled.

TEXT

1 Think about the setting:

a) When does the story take place: in the past, in the present or sometime in the future? Explain how you know this.

b) Where does the story take place: in a town, in a forest or in a village?

c) Look at the picture of the old lady's kitchen. Write a description of the kitchen.

2 Think about the characters:

a) Who are the two main characters in the play?

b) What did you think of the beggar? Give reasons for your answer.

c) What did you think of the old lady? Give reasons for your answer.

d) What is the job of the narrator in the play? (Use a dictionary if you are not sure.)

3 How can you tell that this story is a play?

SENTENCE

1 Copy this play. Punctuate it correctly. Fill in the missing full stops and question marks.

Narrator: The man made some soup It smelt delicious

Lady: It smells lovely

Man: Would you like to try some

Lady: Yes please What sort of soup is it

Man: It is tomato soup

Lady: Tomato soup is my favourite flavour

Narrator: The man put some soup in a bowl

Lady: This soup tastes delicious May I have some more

2 Continue the conversation in the form of a play and punctuate it correctly.

WORD

1 Copy these sentences. Underline the words that contain the same letter patterns. Then find a word in the play *Nail Soup* with the same letter pattern.
Do it like this: I slipped on the <u>ice</u> tw<u>ice</u>. n<u>ice</u>

a) I looked around and found a pound.

b) The queen went to town wearing her crown.

c) You cannot peep when you are asleep.

d) The king lost his ring.

e) Be careful not to tread on my head.

2 Think of two more words which contain the same phonemes as each of these:

a) s<u>ou</u>p   *b)* b<u>oi</u>l   *c)* k<u>i</u>nd   *d)* p<u>oo</u>r   *e)* g<u>oo</u>d

15

Story starter

Use this story starter to get you going.

Think of an exciting middle and ending for the story.

Crash! I woke up suddenly when I heard the noise downstairs. My heart was thumping. What could it be? I got out of bed and walked slowly down the stairs…

Story ending

Here is an idea to help you continue a story you have read.

Write an ending to *The Sandcastle* in Unit 1.1.

◆ Has Gran really got any flags in her bag?

◆ What happens next?

◆ What does Josie say? (Remember to start a new line whenever anyone speaks and to use speech marks.)

◆ Imagine a big wave crashes over Josie's sandcastle when she has finished it!

Story settings

Describe your bedroom at home. Is it big? small? light? dark? How is it decorated? What furniture is in it? Is it tidy?

Chips (in Unit 1.4) is always getting into trouble. Make up a story about a bad day he had when he helped his Mum clean his bedroom. What sort of things could go wrong?

Shape poems

- Look back to Unit 1.2.
- On a piece of paper draw a large outline of either a hedgehog, a spider or a butterfly.
- Inside the shape write in rough lots of interesting words or sentences to describe the way the creature looks, moves or some of the things it does.
- When you have finished, decide which bits you want to keep or to change.
- Do you want to add anything?
- Check your spellings.
- When you are happy with what you have written, make a best copy and decorate it.

Plays

Write the story of *The Sandcastle* Unit 1.1 as a playscript. Begin it like this:

Narrator: Josie Smith is on holiday at the seaside. Josie has just finished building a sandcastle. She has spent all her money on a windmill for her sister, but what she really wants is some flags for her own sandcastle.

Josie: It's finished.

Gran: What's the matter? Are you wishing you still had your spending money?

Handy hints for writing stories

Setting

Where will your story take place?

- in a house?
- in a shop?
- in a wood?
- in a hospital?
- at the seaside?
- at school?
- somewhere else?

Characters

- Who will be in your story?
- What will they look like?
- What sort of things will they do?
- What sort of things will they say?

Plot

- What will your story be about?
- How will it begin?
- What sort of things will happen in the middle?
- Give your story a good ending.

How are you getting on with the things in the chart?

If you need extra practice try the activities shown.

Grammar and punctuation	Ways of introducing dialogue	1
	Using verb tenses correctly	2
	Writing sentences that make sense	3
	Capital letters, full stops and question marks	4
Spelling, phonics and vocabulary	Prefixes	5
	Syllables	6
	Spelling strategies	7
	Phonemes	8

1 Write as many words as you can think of that you can use when someone is speaking. Do it like this: said, shouted, whispered

2 Read this story about a fire.

There *is* a big fire along our road. I *hear* the sound of the fire engines. They *come* round the corner very fast. The firefighters *jump* down. They *get* out the hoses and *aim* them at the flames. Someone *is* trapped in the house! The firefighters *tell* the man to jump. He *leaps* from the window. The firefighters *catch* him in a big blanket. It *is* very exciting!

Now rewrite the story as if the fire happened yesterday. Change the verbs so they make sense. Do it like this: Yesterday there was a big fire along our road.

3 Copy these sentences.
Think of a suitable word to fill in each gap.

a) Before you _____ to bed you _____ your teeth.

b) The _____ lady was carrying a _____ bag.

c) The _____ wagged its _____ happily.

d) I had _____ soup and _____ sandwich for my tea.

e) When Emma and Tom got home _____ took off _____ muddy shoes.

f) Abdi whispered _____ but Shireen shouted _____ .

4 Copy these sentences and punctuate them correctly.

a) the old man sat down on the bench to rest

b) where is my pencil it is on top of the table

c) what colour is an apple it can be green or red

d) do you know the names of all the days of the week

e) when is it time to go home school finishes at half past three

5 Take the prefix off each of these words. Write the words you are left with.

a) undo   *b)* disappear   *c)* disagree   *d)* untie

e) undress   *f)* distrust   *g)* unbuckle   *h)* displease

i) unload   *j)* disobey

6 Copy these words with two syllables. Do it like this: magnet – mag/net

a) slowly   *b)* beggar   *c)* snowflake   *d)* hugging

e) butter   *f)* spelling   *g)* careful   *h)* report   *i)* undo

j) picture

7 *a)* Choose 10 words you need to learn from the back cover of this book. Use the *Look, say, cover, write, check* method to help you learn them. Use the *Handy hints for spelling* to help.

b) When you can spell the words make up some sentences and use the words in them.

8 Divide each group of words into two sets according to their phonemes.

a) heat, feel, lead, reading, asleep, street, seated, freedom, greedy, hearing

b) boat, window, below, shown, float, road, soap, growing, cloak, slowed

c) moon, chew, news, room, school, grew, flew, looping, broom, screws

Handy hints for spelling

◆ Is the word spelt as it sounds? Does it contain any phonemes you already know?

◆ Does the word look right? Do you know any other words like it?

◆ Can you break the word into smaller parts? Which is the most difficult part of the word?

◆ Do you know what the word means?

◆ Have you used a word book or dictionary to help you?

LOOK   SAY   COVER   WRITE   CHECK

The Noise in the Night

The middle of the night, and everyone in the house asleep. Everyone? Then what was that noise?

Creak! and then, after a pause, Creak! And then, Creak!...

Mrs Sparrow heard it. The noise woke her, as the crying of her children would have woken her. But this was someone else's job. She nudged her husband. She nudged and nudged until Bill Sparrow stirred, groaned. He had been dreaming of the garden.

"Bill!" she whispered. "Come on! Wake up!"

"Yes," he said. "Just a minute, and I'll do that."

"Listen."

Creak! and then, Creak! And then, Creak!

"Can't you hear it?"

"Yes."

"What is it?"

"I don't know."

"But it's in the house!"

"Yes, it is."

"Downstairs!"

"Yes."

"Bill, what are you going to do about it?"

He nearly said again, "I don't know." Then he pulled himself together. He tried to think clearly what he ought to do. First he

ought to wake up properly. Then, he ought to get up. He ought to find out what was making that noise that bothered Alice so. That was it: find out.

"I'm getting up," he said out aloud. "I'm going to find out about that row downstairs."

He reached for the pencil torch that Mrs Sparrow kept under her pillow. He wouldn't switch on the lights; he wouldn't even use the torch until he had to. He would surprise whatever it was. Whoever it was.

From The Battle of Bubble and Squeak *by Philippa Pearce*

TEXT

1 Answer the questions below. Write down the words from the passage that contain the answer. Set your work out like this:

My answer	Words from the passage
a) The story takes place at night.	The middle of the night

a) When did the story take place?

b) Where were Mr and Mrs Sparrow?

c) What woke up Mrs Sparrow?

d) What sort of noise was it?

e) Where was the noise coming from?

2 How do you think Mr and Mrs Sparrow felt? Explain your answer.

3 How does the author try to make you feel when you read the passage?

4 What noises can you hear lying in bed at night before you go to sleep?

SENTENCE

In some places in the passage the writer has left out the name of the person who is speaking. Copy out five things from the passage that you think Mrs Sparrow said. Then do the same for Mr Sparrow. Remember to put in the speech marks and punctuate each sentence correctly. Begin like this:

"Listen," whispered Mrs Sparrow.

WORD

1 Think of a word that rhymes with each of the words below. Check your spellings in a dictionary.

a) table   *b)* candle   *c)* tumble   *d)* twinkle   *e)* simple

2 What do all the words in question 1 have in common?

3 Write the words in the list below:

**wobble   cliff   muffle   nettle   haggle
kettle   straggle   hobble   fiddle   scuffle**

4 What do you notice about the consonants in the middle of each word in question 3?

5 Make up 10 sentences. Use some of the words from question 1 and question 3 in them.

Using a Dictionary and a Thesaurus

A dictionary

A dictionary gives you the meaning, or definition, of a word. Sometimes there may be more than one definition for each word.
A dictionary is arranged in alphabetical order like this:

fox a wild animal that looks like a dog and has a long, furry tail
fraction **1.** a number that is not a whole number e.g. 1/2 **2.** a very small part of something
fragile easily broken
fraud a trick, or a person who tries to cheat someone
free **1.** with nothing to stop you doing something or going somewhere **2.** not costing anything e.g. a *free* gift
freeze **1.** to change into ice **2.** to be very cold

A thesaurus

A thesaurus gives you a list of synonyms for each word – other words that mean the same thing. A thesaurus is also arranged in alphabetical order.

This thesaurus tells you whether the word is:
a noun (n.),
a verb (v.)
or an adjective (adj.).
These are printed in *italics*.

This thesaurus sometimes gives you the opposite of the word.
The opposites are printed in blue.

foxy *adj.* cunning, crafty, artful, sly, canny artless
fraction *n.* portion, part, fragment, piece whole
fragile *adj.* weak, delicate, brittle, frail sturdy, strong
fraud *n.* trickery, swindle, deception, deceit honesty
free **1.** *adj.* gratis, complimentary, without charge **2.** *adj.* liberated, independent **3.** *adj.* loose, untied **4.** *v.* dismiss, release, acquit enslave
freeze *v.* refrigerate, chill melt, thaw

TEXT

1 What is a dictionary used for?

2 What is a thesaurus used for?

3 How are the words in a dictionary and thesaurus arranged?

4 What is another word for 'the meaning of a word'?

5 What do we call words that have the same meaning?

6 Use the extract from the dictionary to answer these questions.

   a) What is the definition of 'fragile'?

   b) Which words have more than one definition?

7 Use the extract from the thesaurus to answer these questions.

   a) Write some synonyms for 'foxy'.

   b) Which two words are nouns?

   c) What is the opposite of fraud?

   d) Which word has four different uses?

SENTENCE

1 Copy these sentences. Underline the verb in each sentence.

   a) The fox ran fast.

   b) Cows eat grass.

   c) The lady carried her bag.

   d) The man hooted his horn.

   e) Birds sing in the trees.

   f) The flag fluttered in the breeze.

   g) I drank the cup of tea.

   h) The shark swam under the water.

   i) You write with a pencil.

   j) The queen sat on the throne.

2 Now write each sentence again but miss out the verb.

3 Copy and complete this: every sentence must have a v _ _ _ . A sentence does not make s _ _ _ _ if the v _ _ _ is missing.

WORD

1 Rewrite these sentences. Replace the underlined word with a suitable synonym.

   a) The fox was a <u>crafty</u> animal.   b) The glass vase was very <u>fragile</u>.

   c) The judge decided to <u>free</u> the prisoner.

2 Use a dictionary or thesaurus to help you with these questions.

   a) Which of the words below mean the same as 'evil'?

   wicked   safe   sinful   wrong   strong

   b) Write three synonyms for each of these words. **nice   small   said**

3 Arrange these nouns in alphabetical order.

   a) chair, sausage, picture   b) pencil, jelly, lamp, water

   c) desk, computer, window, flower   d) secret, sleeve, soap, smile

4 a) Write the days of the week in alphabetical order.

   b) Now do the same for the months of the year.

Under the Sea

Did you know…

- that over half the world is covered with water?
- that a group of fish is called a school?
- that there are some deep parts of the ocean that have never been explored?

1 There are millions of tiny plants and animals living under the sea that are so small you can't see them unless you use a microscope. These are called plankton. Lots of fish eat these plants and animals.

2 Whales are the largest living animals. The Blue Whale can grow up to 33 metres in length and weigh up to 200 tonnes (as much as 200 small cars!). Whales need to come up to the surface to breathe occasionally.

3 Dolphins need to come to the surface to breathe too. Dolphins are very intelligent creatures. They can 'talk' to each other in a kind of 'sound' language.

4 Many people are afraid of sharks. They look fierce and can swim very fast. They have very sharp teeth and strong jaws.

5 An octopus has eight legs called tentacles. These have suction pads on them which the octopus uses to catch crabs and small fish.

6 Plants and weeds grow in the sea just as they do on land. Most of them only grow where the water is shallow because they need sunlight to help them grow.

TEXT

1 Write one fact from each paragraph that you feel is most important.

2 Think of a good title for each paragraph. For example: 1 Plankton

3 *a)* Is the passage opposite fiction or non-fiction?

b) Do you think it is true? Say why.

4 Write out these statements again in two sets – one set about fiction books and the other about non-fiction books.

Fiction books are made up.

They are not always true.

Non-fiction books contain facts and information.

Fiction books are usually about a series of things that happen to a particular character.

Non-fiction books may contain maps, diagrams or charts.

You usually read a fiction book from beginning to end.

You don't have to read information books all the way through. You can just pick the bit you want to read.

SENTENCE

1 Copy these sentences. Fill in the gaps with sensible verbs.

a) Lots of fish _____ plankton.

b) Whales _____ to the surface.

c) Dolphins _____ to each other.

d) Sharks _____ very fast.

e) Sharks _____ fierce.

f) An octopus _____ tentacles.

g) Plants _____ sunlight.

2 Copy and complete this sentence: A verb is a _____ word.

3 Say what each of these groups of verbs all have in common. Use a dictionary if necessary. Do it like this: 'say', 'whisper' and 'speak' all mean to 'talk'.

a) munch, consume, chew

b) race, chase, sprint

c) slither, crawl, slide

d) rise, mount, ascend

WORD

1 Add the suffix 'ing' to the verbs below, like this: pick – picking
a) eat   *b)* look   *c)* talk   *d)* see   *e)* need   *f)* suck

2 Add the suffix 'ing' to these verbs, like this: make – making
a) save   *b)* come   *c)* use   *d)* take   *e)* smile   *f)* ride

3 Write a sentence and say what you notice about the changes you had to make to the verbs in question 2 when you added 'ing'.

4 Add the suffix 'ing' to these verbs, like this: swim – swimming
a) hop   *b)* sit   *c)* bat   *d)* bet   *e)* cut   *f)* beg

5 Write a sentence and say what you notice about the changes you had to make to the verbs in question 4 when you added 'ing'.

Inside a Castle

This drawing comes from a book called *All About Castles*. This is the contents page of the book. ▶

All about Castles

Contents

There was no glass in the windows. Castles were very draughty.

The private bedrooms were for the lord's family and special guests.

The main hall was heated by a large fire. The hall was used for eating, entertaining and for everyday business. At night, most people slept in here, too!

Fresh water was drawn from the well.

All the food and drink and other supplies were kept in the stores.

The moat was a deep ditch of water. It helped to keep enemies out.

The castle drawbridge was put down to let people in.

TEXT

1 *a)* Where did the lord and his family live? *b)* What was the main hall used for?
c) Where did fresh water come from? *d)* What was kept in the stores?
e) Why were castles draughty? *f)* How did the drawbridge and moat help to protect the castle?

2 How is the information on page 26 presented?
a) as a page of writing *b)* in a chart *c)* as a list *d)* as a picture with labels

3 What is the title of the book from which the drawing came?

4 On which page of that book would you find:
a) the drawing *b)* something about ghosts
c) information on how to build a castle?

5 Explain what a contents page is and where you would find it in a book.

SENTENCE

Write these sentences again. Put in the missing commas. The first sentence has been done for you.

a) The castle was cold, dark, gloomy and draughty.
b) The main hall was used for eating entertaining business and sleeping.
c) Food drink weapons and armour were kept in the store.
d) The castle was protected by high walls a moat and a drawbridge.
e) The soup was made with tomatoes onions potatoes and carrots.
f) My favourite colours are red yellow green and blue.
g) I bought a pencil a book a badge and a rubber at the shop.
h) On holiday I visited France Germany Italy and Spain.

WORD

1 Find these words on the page opposite. Check if they are spelt correctly or not. Then write down all the words correctly.

a) famaly *b)* glass *c)* windows
d) castel *e)* hall *f)* fire
g) evryday *h)* nite *i)* pepol
j) living *k)* drink *l)* book
m) drawn *n)* large *o)* warter
p) helpt *q)* drafty *r)* kept

2 Write down the meaning of each of these words. If you are not sure, look them up in a dictionary.

a) castle *b)* guest *c)* private
d) servant *e)* moat *f)* drawbridge

The Conjuror

Conjuror: Good afternoon, my friends.
My name is Mr E.

Stuart: That's a stupid name.

Rachel: What does the E stand for?

Conjuror: Aha, it's a mystery.

Mum: Mystery, Mister E – I see! Now children, sit and watch Mr E's show and then you can all have tea.
(Children sit on the floor.)

Conjuror: Now, my friends, my magic wand is telling me that one of you has a birthday today.

Stuart: I bet it was my mum who told you, not your wand at all.

Conjuror: It's you, isn't it? You're the one.

Stuart: So what?

Conjuror: I am inviting you to help me perform Trick One.

Stuart: I don't want to.

Conjuror: Very well, I shall choose again. What is your name, young friend?

Rachel: Rachel.

Conjuror: Would you like to help me perform Trick One?

Rachel: Yes please.

Conjuror: Then step forward and hold this hat while I wave my wand. Would our other friends like to help me say the magic spell?

Children: Yes!

Stuart: No!

Conjuror: *(Tapping the magic hat)* Very well, repeat after me: Abracadabra and Postman Pat, what's inside the magic hat?

Children: Abracadabra and Postman Pat, what's inside the magic hat?

Conjuror: I'm ready to grab it. I think it's a… *(He puts his hand into the hat and pulls out a rabbit.)*

Children: RABBIT!
(They clap.)

Stuart: That's stupid. Anyone could do that. I bet you couldn't make a monster come out of your hat.

Conjuror: We shall see.

From The Birthday Surprise
by Julia Donaldson

TEXT

1 Think about the setting of the story.

a) Where does the story take place? Write and explain how you know this.

b) Imagine you are one of the children. Describe some of the things you see and do at the party.

2 Think about the characters.

a) Name the characters in the play.

b) What sort of boy is Stuart? How would you describe him?

c) How can you tell when a different person starts speaking in the play?

3 Think about the plot.

a) The instructions which tell the actors what to do are written in brackets like this: (*Children sit on the floor.*) Find and write down the instructions which tell the children and the conjuror what to do.

b) What do you think might happen at the end of the play? Write a few more lines of the play and continue the story.

SENTENCE

We can divide sentences into different types.

1 Find and write down all the questions you can find in the play.

2 Find and write down all the exclamations.

3 Find and write down all the orders.

4 Find and write down five statements.

WORD

1 The phonemes in these words from the play all sound the same: ag<u>ai</u>n s<u>ay</u> w<u>ave</u>.

pain   clay   today   cave   stain saved   crayon   braver   raining stayed   grave   against   sprain saint

Copy the grid and write the words from the list above in the correct columns.

'ai' words	'ay' words	'ave' words

2 Copy the grid below and write three more words in each column that contain the same phoneme.

myst<u>e</u>ry	s<u>ee</u>	t<u>ea</u>

29

Labelling a picture

In your book write a label for each part of the bike that is numbered. Explain what each thing is used for. Do it like this:

4 This is the bell. You ring this to warn people you are coming.

saddle   brakes   handlebar   bell   chain   pedal

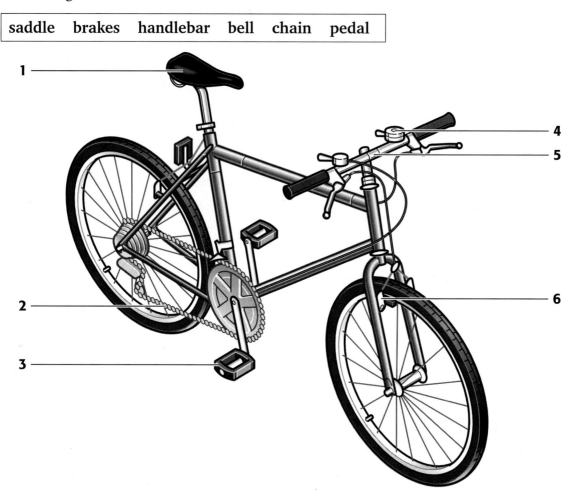

Presenting information in a chart

Copy this chart in your book. Use the information from Unit 1.9 to help you.

Explain how different parts of the castle were used.

The drawbridge	This was used to let people in or keep people out.
The moat	
The main hall	
The stores	
The bedrooms	

Writing reports

Imagine Smudge is your dog. You are going on holiday. Write some notes for a friend who is going to look after her for you.

Write a paragraph on each of these things.

1 Exercise (to keep her healthy)
2 Food (giving Smudge the right food)
3 Grooming (keeping her clean)

Do it like this:

Exercise

It is important that Smudge has enough exercise to keep her fit. She needs at least one walk each day. Sometimes it is good to let her have a lovely long walk in a park or the countryside. Smudge likes to play in the garden as often as possible.

Stuart's party

Copy and complete this report on what happened at Stuart's party (Unit 1.10). Finish the report when Mr E pulled a rabbit out of the hat.

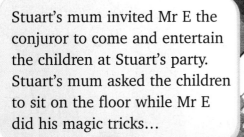

Stuart's mum invited Mr E the conjuror to come and entertain the children at Stuart's party. Stuart's mum asked the children to sit on the floor while Mr E did his magic tricks…

Sentences

◆ Do your sentences make sense?

Punctuation

◆ Have you punctuated it correctly with capital letters, full stops, question marks, exclamation marks and commas?

Spelling

◆ Have you checked for silly spelling mistakes?
◆ Have you looked up any words you are not sure of?

Handwriting

◆ Is your handwriting easy to read?
◆ Are you going to do your work on the computer?

How are you getting on with the things in the chart? If you need extra practice try the activities shown.

Grammar and punctuation	Speech marks	1
	Different types of sentences	2
	Verbs	3
	Commas (in lists)	4
Spelling, phonics and vocabulary	'le' words	5
	Synonyms	6
	Verbs ending in 'ing'	7
	Phonemes	8
	Spelling strategies	9

a)

Why haven't you been to see me lately?

I haven't been well!

b)

What did the robber say to the weight-lifter?

This is a hold-up!

c)

Where did you learn to drive?

CRASH!

I took a crash course!

1 Copy these sentences and fill in what each person said.

a) " _____ " asked the doctor.

   " _____ " replied the man.

b) The weight-lifter asked, " _____ "

   The robber answered, " _____ "

c) " _____ " asked the police officer.

   " _____ " the motorist replied.

2 Copy and punctuate these sentences correctly. Say whether each sentence is a statement, a question, an order or an exclamation.

a) how much did your coat cost

b) wow that is expensive

c) let me try the coat on

d) the coat fits me very nicely

3 Copy the sentences. Correct the underlined verbs.

a) The boy <u>hurted</u> his knee.

b) I <u>seen</u> him yesterday.

c) She <u>give</u> me some crisps.

d) The children <u>done</u> some sums.

e) The house was <u>shook</u> by an explosion.

f) The leaves <u>was</u> falling.

4 Copy these sentences. Put in the missing commas.

a) In the park we saw dogs cats ducks and squirrels.

b) At the shop I got some apples pears oranges and bananas.

c) Tom likes curry spaghetti pizzas and hamburgers.

d) In his tool kit the man had a hammer a saw a screwdriver and a drill.

5 Write these sets of 'le' words in alphabetical order.

a) circle bundle handle dangle gurgle

b) ladle rifle stumble tangle jangle

c) middle bubble fizzle cuddle little hassle

6 Write these synonyms in pairs, according to meaning.

enormous hoax abandon smooth weak leave feeble sleek trick huge

7 Add 'ing' to these verbs. Make any changes needed.

a) watch   *b)* hug   *c)* bake   *d)* tap   *e)* bite   *f)* draw

g) write   *h)* pin

8 Copy and underline the phoneme in each of these words. Add some more words to each list containing the same phonemes. Use a dictionary to check.

a) claw, door, caught, short, more

b) cow, sound, allow, crown, loud, pouch

c) chair, care, pear, wear, stare, fair

9 *a)* Write the names of the months of the year in your book. Check their spellings at the back of this book.

b) Use the *Look, say, cover, write, check* method to help you learn those that you got wrong.

Handy hints for spelling

♦ Is the word spelt as it sounds? Does it contain any phonemes you already know?

♦ Does the word look right? Do you know any other words like it?

♦ Can you break the word into smaller parts? Which is the most difficult part of the word?

♦ Do you know what the word means?

♦ Have you used a word book or dictionary to help you?

Dreamtime

This is a creation story about how the world began. It is a story told by Aborigines in Australia.

At the beginning of the world, in Dreamtime, it was dark. Nothing grew. Nothing moved. Everything was still and quiet. All the birds, animals and reptiles were still asleep under the ground.

Then one day, the Rainbow Serpent woke up and came to the surface. She began to have a look around. She was so huge that wherever she crawled she left behind a winding track. Wherever she stopped to sleep she left a deep hollow in the ground.

After a while the Rainbow Serpent got lonely. She wanted some company. She wanted someone to talk to. She decided to wake up all the other creatures.

The big-bellied frogs were the first to wake up. Their stomachs were full of water they had stored. They were so fat they could hardly hop. They looked so funny it made the Rainbow Serpent laugh to see them.

The world was a dry and barren place at this time. There were no rivers or lakes so no plants or trees could grow. As the Rainbow Serpent looked at the frogs she had an idea. She tickled the frogs' fat bellies with her forked tongue. At first it had no effect and then they began to smile. And then they began to giggle. And then they began to snigger. And then they began to howl with laughter. They laughed and laughed so much that the water inside them started to gush out everywhere. It began to fill the tracks and hollows left by the Rainbow Serpent. And still the water kept gushing out until all the rivers, lakes and seas in the world were formed.

Gradually plants and trees began to shoot up and grow where nothing had grown before. Instead of just brown rocks and sand the world became full of colour. One by one the creatures woke up and came sleepily up from under the ground.

At first the animals all got on well together. The world was a happy place. Everyone lived together in peace and harmony. But then things started to go wrong and they began to argue and fight and fall out with each other.

A traditional Australian story

TEXT

1 Who is the main character in the story?

2 Write the main events in the story. Do it like this: In the beginning …

3 Why did things start to go wrong?

4 Draw some pictures showing an argument between two animals that might have taken place. Include speech bubbles to show what they said to each other.

5 What is a 'creation' story?

6 Why do you think the story is called *Dreamtime*?

7 Is the story true? Give a reason for your answer.

SENTENCE

1 Copy these sentences and underline the two nouns in each.

a) The frogs had fat bellies.   *b)* A rock is made of hard stone.
c) The bridge is across the river.   *d)* A bird has wings to help it fly.

2 Find five nouns in the story and write them down.

3 Think of a good noun to finish these phrases.

a) a dark _____   *b)* a windy _____   *c)* the heavy _____
d) some big _____   *e)* my best _____   *f)* the tall _____

4 Draw a chart like this. Write the names of five different nouns in each column.

things to write with	things you read	things you eat

WORD

1 Write the plural of each of the nouns below. Do it like this: one bird but two birds.

a) bird   *b)* animal   *c)* plant   *d)* tree   *e)* lake   *f)* river

2 What did you do to each noun to make it plural?

3 Write the plural of each of the nouns below. Do it like this: one fox but two foxes.

a) fox   *b)* dish   *c)* church   *d)* brush   *e)* bunch   *f)* box

4 Copy and complete this rule.

Add _____ to nouns that end in 'ch', 'sh', 'ss' or 'x' to change them into the plural.

5 Write the singular of each of these nouns like this: lots of tables but only one table.

a) lots of friends   *b)* lots of monkeys   *c)* lots of brushes   *d)* lots of foxes

How the Squirrel got its Stripes

Long ago in India Lord Rama lived with his beautiful wife, Sita. Nearby on the island of Sri Lanka lived Rawana, a wicked Demon King. One day Rawana kidnapped Sita and carried her off to his island. Lord Rama asked the monkeys to help him build a bridge to the island and rescue his wife.

The monkeys worked very hard. They carried piles of rocks every day to build the bridge. Suddenly, one monkey noticed a small squirrel who was also helping.

"What are you trying to do?" he laughed.

"I'm helping Rama to build his bridge," the squirrel replied.

"But you are too small to help," smiled the monkey.

"No, I'm not," answered the squirrel. "I can bring little pebbles."

Then all the other monkeys began to laugh and told the squirrel not to be so silly. They told her to go back home and leave the work to them.

But the little squirrel took no notice and just carried on as before. One monkey got angry, grabbed hold of her tail and threw her out of the way. She went flying into the air but when she came down Lord Rama caught her. He had overheard everything.

He held the squirrel gently and called all the monkeys to gather round. He told the monkeys that they should not have behaved in such a way.

"Even weak, tiny creatures can show their love, and can serve in different ways," he said. Then he stooped down and put the squirrel on the ground. "Little one," he said softly, "you have loved and served me well." Then he stroked the squirrel on her back and left his finger marks for all to see.

Still, to this very day, the Indian squirrel has three white stripes on its back where it was once stroked by Lord Rama.

An Indian legend

TEXT

1 *a)* What job did the monkeys have to do? *b)* Who gave them the job?
c) Why were they given the job?

2 Why did the monkeys laugh at the squirrel?

3 How do you think the squirrel felt when she was laughed at?

4 What do you think of: *a)* the monkeys' behaviour towards the squirrel?
b) the way Lord Rama treated her?

5 Do you think this story is true? Give a reason.

6 Did you enjoy the story? Say what you liked or didn't like.

7 Which of these would make the best moral for the story:

a) Everyone is special. *b)* It's the thought that counts.
c) Everyone can help, whatever their size or strength. *d)* Every little helps.

SENTENCE

1 Find and write down five nouns from the story.

2 Copy these sentences and underline the noun in each.

a) The dog chased the stick. *b)* The boy kicked the ball.
c) The cat chased a bird. *d)* The man got into his car.

3 Rewrite the sentences in question 2. Change the nouns into the plural.
Do it like this: *a)* The dogs chased the sticks.

Think carefully about any other changes you will have to make!

4 Think of a suitable collective noun to complete each of these phrases.
a) a pile of stones *b)* a _____ of sheep *c)* a _____ of bananas

5 Think of a way of finishing these phrases.

a) a team of _____ *b)* a gang of _____ *c)* a swarm of_____

WORD

1 Copy and complete these charts.

2 Add three words to each set.

3 Make up a rule for each set, explaining how to change the singular nouns into the plural form.

singular	plural
lady	ladies
baby	
	flies
city	cities
	fairies
lorry	

singular	plural
leaf	leaves
wife	
loaf	
	halves
	lives
thief	

4 Write the plural of these nouns. Take care! *a)* woman *b)* child *c)* foot
d) sheep *e)* tooth *f)* goose

Foxy Fables

The Greedy Fox

One day a clever fox saw a shepherd putting his dinner inside a hollow tree before setting out to look after his flock of sheep. When the shepherd was out of sight the fox ran over to the tree. The gap in the trunk was very narrow, but by pulling in his sides the fox managed to squeeze inside.

Once he was in the tree, the fox gobbled up the food until every bit was gone. Then he tried to get out of the tree again. To his horror he found that he had eaten so much that his stomach had grown plump. No matter how hard he tried he could not squeeze back out again. Now when the fox realised he was trapped he began to howl. One of his friends, who was passing by, came to see what the matter was. "There's nothing I can do," he said. "You'll just have to wait until you grow thin enough to get out again. I hope the shepherd doesn't return before then!"

The greedy fox was annoyed with himself for being so silly.

Moral: We should think before we act.

The Crafty Fox

One day a crow was sitting on a branch of a tree holding a piece of cheese in her beak. She was just getting ready to eat the cheese when a hungry fox looked up and saw her. The fox put on his best smile and said, "Hello Mrs Crow. How lovely you look today." The crow was very pleased and nodded her head but said nothing.

"Oh my! I bet you are a beautiful singer. I am so tired I would like to rest under your tree. Can you sing me to sleep?" Now when the crow heard the fox's praise she was very flattered. As she began to sing she let go of the cheese and it fell to the ground. The fox immediately jumped on it and gobbled it up. He smiled up at the crow and politely said, "Thank you!" The hungry crow was annoyed with herself for being so silly.

Moral: Beware of flattery. It may not be meant.

Aesop's Fables

TEXT

1 Was the fox in the first fable clever or foolish? Say why.

2 Rewrite these sentences in order so they tell the first fable.

The fox grew fat and could not get out of the tree again.

The fox squeezed into the hole in the tree.

A shepherd left his dinner in a hollow tree.

The greedy fox ate all the food.

3 What do you think happens at the end of the first fable?

4 Which animal was foolish in the second fable? Say why.

5 How would you describe the fox in the second fable?

6 Explain what you think the moral at the end of each fable means.

7 What do you notice about the way both fables begin and end?

8 Explain what you think a moral is. Use a dictionary if you need help.

SENTENCE

1 Copy these sentences and write a suitable adjective in each gap.

One day a _____ fox saw a shepherd putting his dinner inside a _____ tree. The gap in the tree was very _____ .
After the fox ate the food his stomach was _____ .

2 Find two adjectives in the second fable that describe:

a) the fox   *b)* the crow

3 Copy these descriptions and underline the adjective in each one.

a) a hungry girl   *b)* the angry dog   *c)* a closed door   *d)* some green leaves

4 Think of a sensible adjective to go with each of these nouns.

a) the _____ giant   *b)* a _____ bag   *c)* some _____ trees

5 Find and write the pairs of adjectives that mean the opposite of each other.

WORD

1 In the word 'shepherd' we do not say the second 'h'. It is a silent letter.

Choose either 'kn' or 'wr' to begin each of these words. Use a dictionary to help you.

a) _ _ ow   *b)* _ _ ee   *c)* _ _ ite   *d)* _ _ ap   *e)* _ _ ock

2 Write down two more words that begin with 'kn' and 'wr'.

3 Write these words in two groups according to their silent letters.

comb   thumb   fasten   rustle   whistle   lamb   castle   listen   bomb

4 Find and write some words which contain a silent 'u' (as in 'guess').
Use a dictionary to help you. (Clue: The words often begin with 'g'.)

Little Red Riding Hood

One day Little Red Riding Hood went to see her grandmother. On her way she stopped to pick some flowers. Just then a wolf passed by.

As soon as Little Red Riding Hood had gone, the wolf took a shortcut to grandmother's house. He grabbed the old lady and locked her in a shed.

The wolf dressed in grandmother's clothes, jumped into bed and waited for Little Red Riding Hood.

When she arrived, she thought her 'grandmother' looked strange.

The nearer she got, the stranger 'grandmother' looked.

As soon as she saw the sharp, pointed teeth, she knew that it was the wicked wolf pretending to be grandmother.

Little Red Riding Hood jumped out of the window and ran into the woods.

A woodcutter caught the wolf by the tail and tied him up.

Just then, they heard some cries coming from the shed, and there they found the real grandmother safe and sound. They pushed the wicked wolf into the shed until they decided what to do with him.

TEXT

1 Who are the four main characters in the story?

2 Who is *a)* the villain?
b) the hero or heroine?

3 Who was weak and helpless in the story?

4 Describe Red Riding Hood. Write some sentences about: *a)* how she looked (her appearance and what she wore) *b)* the sort of girl she was (e.g. Was she... kind? foolish? brave? etc.)

5 What do you think of the wolf? Explain your answer.

6 What do you think Little Red Riding Hood and the wolf were thinking the first time they met each other?

7 Do you feel sorry for grandmother? Give your reasons.

8 Do you feel sorry for the wolf? Give your reasons.

9 What might the woodcutter have thought when he heard someone crying for help?

SENTENCE

1 Write down which of these adjectives you could use about the wolf.

**good   evil   strong   weak   frightening   crafty   cruel
kind   tricky   sly   nasty   horrible   foolish   bad**

2 Sort the adjectives below into three sets of colour, size and feeling.

**huge   unhappy   enormous   tired   white   tall   golden   tiny
dark   grey   nervous   hungry   small   green   frightened**

3 Now think of three more adjectives to write in each set.

4 Write five sentences and include some of the adjectives from your chart in them.

WORD

1 Add the suffixes 'er' and 'est' to these adjectives, e.g. small – smaller – smallest
a) bright   *b)* dull   *c)* rough   *d)* smooth   *e)* old   *f)* young

2 Add the suffixes 'er' and 'est' to these adjectives, e.g. hot – hotter – hottest
a) big   *b)* fat   *c)* thin   *d)* red   *e)* wet   *f)* sad

3 Write and say what you noticed when you added the suffixes in question 2.

4 Add the suffixes 'er' and 'est' to these adjectives, e.g. busy – busier – busiest
a) lucky   *b)* noisy   *c)* heavy   *d)* jolly   *e)* sorry   *f)* pretty

5 Write and say what you noticed when you added the suffixes in question 4.

Poems to Perform

Down in the park
I met a boy called Fred.
Fred said, "I can't play now,
I'm going home to bed."

Down in the park
I met a girl called Jane.
Jane said, "I've got my wellies
    with me
Just in case of rain!"

TEN little children
Standing in a line,
One fell over a cliff
And then there were NINE.

NINE little children
At the school gate,
Along came a roaring lion
And then there were EIGHT.

EIGHT little children
Travelling to Devon,
One vanished in a puff of smoke
And then there were SEVEN.

I met a Horse as I went walking;
We got talking,
Horse and I.
"Where are you going to, Horse?" I said
(I said to the Horse as he went by).
"Down to the village to get some hay.
Will you come with me?" "No, not I."

I met some Rabbits as I went walking;
We got talking,
Rabbits and I.
"Where are you going to, Rabbits?"
I said
(I said to the Rabbits as they went by).
"Down to the village to get some oats.
Will you come with us?" "No, not I."

From When We Were Very Young *by A. A. Milne*

TEXT

1 *a)* Who did the poet meet in the first poem? *b)* Where were they?

2 *a)* Who did the poet meet in the third poem? *b)* Where were they going?

3 What do you notice about each verse in the second poem?

4 Are the poems opposite rhyming or non-rhyming poems?

5 Find a word in the poems that rhymes with each of these:
   a) Fred   *b)* Jane   *c)* line   *d)* gate   *e)* walking   *f)* by

6 Which is your favourite poem? Explain why.

7 What do you think the title of the page opposite means?

SENTENCE

1 Explain all the different ways in which capital letters are used in the poems opposite.

2 Imagine the third poem was written by a boy called Tom. Write the first verse out as a story, like this: One day, Tom met a horse as he was walking along. Tom began to talk to the horse.

3 Imagine the first poem was written by a girl called Sam. Write the first verse out as a story. Begin like this: One day Sam went to the park.

4 The following sentences don't make sense. Rewrite each one correctly.
   a) Children should always do as they is told.   *b)* Jim had not went far when a lion jump on him.   *c)* I were very hungry.   *d)* His parents was very sad.

WORD

1 The apostrophes in the words below show that some letters are missing. Write the words in full. Do it like this: I'm = I am
   a) I've   *b)* can't   *c)* he's   *d)* we're   *e)* you've   *f)* who's

2 Match up the words in Set A with their partners in Set B. Do it like this: isn't – is not

   SET A   **where's**   **she'll**   **we'd**   **didn't**   **they'd**
   SET B   **we had**   **did not**   **where is**   **they had**   **she will**

3 Write the short form of the words below, like this: that is = that's
   a) would not   *b)* it will   *c)* I am   *d)* we have   *e)* you are

4 Add the suffix 'ful' or 'ly' to each word below, like this; slow ly
   a) hope _____   *b)* quick _____   *c)* care _____   *d)* nice _____
   e) faith _____   *f)* joy _____   *g)* clever _____   *h)* sweet _____

5 Make up some sentences. Use all the words in question 4 in them.

Story starter

Use the beginning of *Dreamtime* (Unit 2.1) to get you going. Think of another way to explain how the mountains and valleys, and the seas and rivers were formed.

Story ending

Continue the *Dreamtime* story. Write an ending to it. Imagine some of the arguments and fights that took place. How did the Rainbow Serpent sort them out? Did they have to make up any rules?

Story sequels

1 Sometimes it is a good idea to use stories you have read to help you write others. Write a story called:

How the _____ got its _____!
(You fill in the blanks).

◆ Lord Rama has asked the monkeys to help him build a bridge.

◆ He wants to cross it to rescue Sita from the wicked Rawana.

◆ Instead of the squirrel helping choose one of these other animals:

a hyena (explain how it got its laugh)

a mouse (explain how it got its long tail)

an elephant (explain how it got its long trunk)

2 Write a Foxy Fable!

Choose one of the sayings below. Make up a foxy fable (like Unit 2.3) to illustrate it.

◆ Look before you leap.

◆ A stitch in time saves nine.

◆ Too many cooks spoil the broth.

Why not tell your story in pictures and words (like Unit 2.4)?

Writing fairy stories and traditional tales

1 List ten fairy stories or traditional stories you know.

2 Choose one story and write about it.

Who was the hero? ◆ Who was the villain?

Where did it take place? ◆ Was there any sort of journey?

Were there dangers ? ◆ How did it end?

3 List five good and five bad characters you might find in fairy stories like:

a beautiful princess

a wicked ogre

a good fairy

a troll

4 Choose one good and one bad character.
Write a description of each one.

What do your characters look like?

Where do they live?

What sort of things do they do?

What sort of things do they say?

Handy hints for writing fairy stories

Setting

Where will your story take place?

◆ in a castle, in a forest, in a cave, on a mountain, in a palace, somewhere else?

Characters

◆ Who will your main characters be?

◆ Who else will be in your story: animals, monsters, other people?

◆ What will they look like?

◆ What will they do?

◆ What will they say?

Plot

◆ What will your story be about?

◆ How will your story begin?

◆ What will happen in the middle?

◆ Will there be a journey, dangers, or problems?

◆ How will the story end – will it be sad? happy? exciting? mysterious?

How are you getting on with the things in the chart? If you need extra practice try the activities shown.

Grammar and punctuation	Nouns – common and collective	1 and 2
	Adjectives	3 and 4
	Sentences make sense	5
Spelling phonics and vocabulary	Singulars and plurals	6 and 7
	Silent letters	8
	Suffixes	9
	Apostrophes	10
	Developing spelling strategies	11 and 12

1 Fill in the gaps with suitable nouns then underline all the nouns in each sentence.

a) The rocket landed on the _____ .

b) The _____ fell and hurt his knee.

c) The caterpillar crawled on the _____ .

d) Monkeys eat _____ .

e) Some _____ wear glasses.

f) A _____ stopped near the shop.

2 Make these into collective nouns.

a) a _____ of wasps   *b)* a _____ of sheep

c) a _____ of bananas   *d)* a _____ of trees

e) a _____ of stamps   *f)* a _____ of sticks

3 Copy and underline the adjectives in these sentences.

a) An orange is round and soft. It has rough skin.

b) Plastic straws are long and hollow.

c) The small glass marble was blue.

d) The noisy dog had a loud bark.

4 Copy this chart. Think of three more adjectives for each column.

size adjectives	colour adjectives	feeling adjectives
tall	grey	annoyed
tiny	silver	jealous

5 Copy the sentences below. Write them as if you were Tom. Do it like this: I was going home.
Tom was going home. On his way he saw an accident. Tom ran home and told his Mum what he had seen.

6 Write the plural of these words:

a) girl *b)* box *c)* knife *d)* city *e)* wish *f)* foot

7 Write the singular of these:

a) toys *b)* arches *c)* babies *d)* leaves *e)* glasses
f) sheep

8 Find and write three words:

a) beginning with 'kn' *b)* beginning with 'gn'
c) ending with 'mb'

9 Add the suffix 'er' and 'est' to these adjectives.

a) cold *b)* big *c)* empty *d)* hot *e)* dry *f)* long

10 Copy these words. Put in the missing apostrophes.

a) isnt *b)* Ive *c)* well *d)* cant *e)* lets *f)* theyre

11 Choose 10 words you need to learn from the back cover of this book. Use the *Look, say, cover, write, check* method to help you learn them.
Use the *Handy hints for spelling* to help.

12 When you can spell the words make up some sentences and use the words in them.

Handy hints for spelling

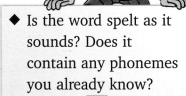

◆ Is the word spelt as it sounds? Does it contain any phonemes you already know?

◆ Does the word look right? Do you know any other words like it?

◆ Can you break the word into smaller parts? Which is the most difficult part of the word?

◆ Do you know what the word means?

◆ Have you used a word book or dictionary to help you?

LOOK SAY COVER WRITE CHECK

Theseus and the Minotaur

King Minos of Crete was protected by a fearsome monster called the Minotaur. It was two metres tall and was half human and half animal. Its head was like a shaggy bull with curved horns as sharp as razors. Its eyes flashed fire. From the neck downwards it was human and had a huge, hairy, barrel chest. The Minotaur did not eat ordinary food. It fed on human flesh!

Now the Minotaur was so savage and dangerous that King Minos kept it hidden in a dark, dank maze of caves and tunnels called the Labyrinth. Each year Minos sent seven boys and seven girls down into the Labyrinth. They were never ever seen again. The people of Crete were terrified that King Minos would choose their children to feed to the Minotaur.

In the end, Princess Ariadne, the daughter of King Minos, took pity on the people. She persuaded Theseus, a young warrior, to climb down into the Labyrinth and get rid of the Minotaur for ever. Ariadne told him to take a ball of wool with him and unwind it as he passed through the maze of tunnels so that he could find his way out again afterwards.

With trembling legs, Theseus began to grope his way through the pitch-dark twisting tunnels. In a short while Theseus heard the snuffling of the monster as it smelt him coming. A blood-chilling roar echoed through the passages as the Minotaur charged. Theseus knew he could never defeat the monster face to face so he decided to trick it. He flattened himself against the cave wall as the beast thundered towards him. Its foul stink filled his nostrils and the ground beneath his feet shook as the monster thundered past him. It passed so close to him that its bristly hair scratched his chest like thorn twigs.

As soon as it had passed him, Theseus struck the Minotaur with his sword. The monster fell in a heap bellowing with fury but Theseus plunged his sword in again and killed the beast.

He threaded his way back to the surface again and was greeted by cheering crowds. The evil king's protector, the Minotaur, was gone for good. They would never be troubled by it again and all their children could sleep safely in their beds once more.

An ancient Greek legend

TEXT

1 What was the name of the beast?

2 Write a description of the Minotaur. Look for clues in the passage. Describe its appearance, where it lived and what it ate.

3 *a)* What was the name of the hero?
b) Write down what you think of him.

4 List all the problems Theseus faced.

5 Explain how Theseus overcame each problem.

6 How do you think Theseus felt when he entered the Labyrinth?

7 What do you think of the ending? Give a reason for your answer.

8 'This story shows how good usually triumphs over evil.' Do you agree with this statement? Say why or why not.

SENTENCE

1 Find and write down three sentences from the passage which include commas.

2 Explain how commas help us when we read.

3 Punctuate these sentences correctly. Use capital letters, full stops, commas, question and exclamation marks where necessary.

a) princess ariadne the daughter of king minos felt sorry for the people

b) she sent theseus a brave warrior down to fight the minotaur

c) the minotaur was a fearsome monster it lived underground

d) do you want to know something horrible the minotaur fed on human flesh

e) holding his sword in his hand theseus went to fight the beast

WORD

1 Sometimes you can find small words hiding in longer words.

The fearsome monster was called the Minotaur.

Copy these words. Find and underline one small word in each word.

a) flashed *b)* human *c)* hairy *d)* ordinary *e)* savage *f)* dangerous
g) children *h)* warrior *i)* down *j)* unwind *k)* began *l)* chilling

2 Write down as many longer words as you can which contain each of these words.

a) ape *b)* eat *c)* own *d)* ear *e)* ale *f)* one

3 Write down your name and the names of four other people in your class. Underline any small words you can find in the names you have written.

4 Write these compound words as word sums like this: fearsome = fear + some.

a) playground *b)* airport *c)* underneath *d)* downstairs *e)* shoelace
f) upon *g)* motorway *h)* runway *i)* scarecrow *j)* below

More poems to perform

Our Family Comes From Around The World

Our family comes
From around the world:
Our hair is straight,
Our hair is curled,
Our eyes are brown,
Our eyes are blue,
Our skins are different
Colours, too.

Tra la tra la
Tra la tra lee
We're one big happy family!

We're girls and boys,
We're big and small,
We're young and old,
We're short and tall.
We're everything
That we can be

Tra la tra la
Tra la tra lee
We're one big happy family!

Mary Ann Hoberman

Rap Connected

We were born to rap
We were born to dance
We were born to sing
We are Queens and Kings
We were born to live de life dat we luv
We were born to luv de life dat we live,
We were born to twist

We were born to shout
We can keep it in
We can hang it out
We got riddim in us mate

Get infected,
Shout it loud,
We are connected.

An extract from 'Rap Connected', by Benjamin Zephaniah

TEXT

1 Find the word that means the opposite of each of these in the first poem:

a) straight   *b)* girls

c) young   *d)* short

2 What do you think the title of the first poem means?

3 What do you notice about the chorus after each verse in the first poem?

4 In what way is the second poem like the first one?

5 What do you think 'we are connected' means?

6 *a)* Why do you think some lines are printed in bold in the second poem?

b) Why do you think some lines are in bigger print than others?

7 What do you notice about the spelling of some words in the second poem? Why do you think they are spelt this way?

SENTENCE

1 What do you notice about the punctuation of the verses in the second poem?

2 Rewrite the first verse of the second poem as if you had written it. Do it like this: I was born to rap.

3 Now rewrite it as if you were talking to another person. Do it like this: You were born to rap.

4 Rewrite these sentences correctly:

a) We was born to dance.

b) We has plenty of hope.

c) Our skins is different.

d) Our family come from around the world.

e) You was wrong.

f) It were raining.

g) I done seven sums in my book.

h) The shoes fits very nicely.

WORD

1 Look in a dictionary. Which letters come about

a) half-way through   *b)* a quarter of the way through

c) three-quarters of the way through?

2 Write a definition for the words below. Use a dictionary to help if necessary.

a) infected   *b)* proud   *c)* snarl   *d)* honest   *e)* detest   *f)* reluctant

3 Now write the words in alphabetical order.

4 Use the *Look, say, cover, write, check* method for learning to spell the words.

5 Arrange some proper nouns in alphabetical order.

a) Choose five boys' names from your class and write them in order.

b) Do the same for five girls' names.

Park Farm

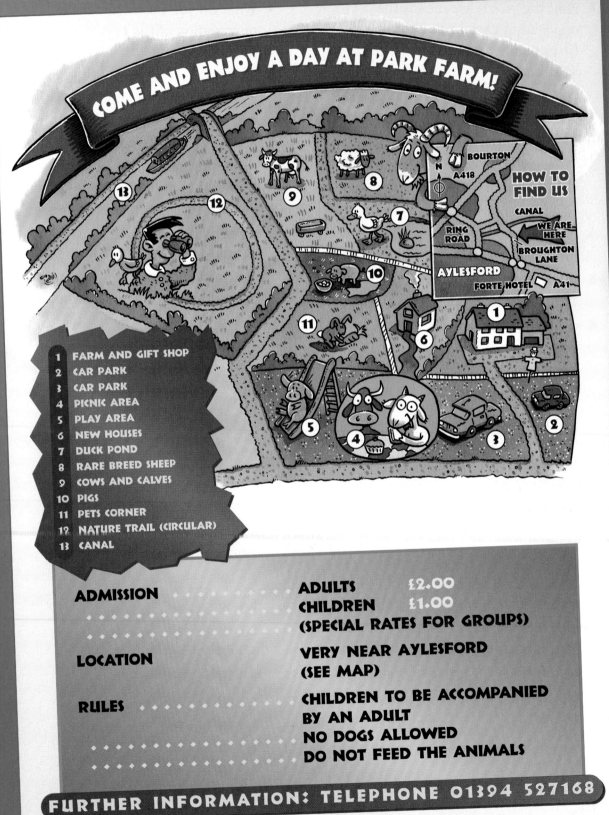

COME AND ENJOY A DAY AT PARK FARM!

1 FARM AND GIFT SHOP
2 CAR PARK
3 CAR PARK
4 PICNIC AREA
5 PLAY AREA
6 NEW HOUSES
7 DUCK POND
8 RARE BREED SHEEP
9 COWS AND CALVES
10 PIGS
11 PETS CORNER
12 NATURE TRAIL (CIRCULAR)
13 CANAL

HOW TO FIND US

BOURTON
A418
N
CANAL
WE ARE HERE
RING ROAD
BROUGHTON LANE
AYLESFORD
FORTE HOTEL
A41

ADMISSION	ADULTS £2.00
	CHILDREN £1.00
	(SPECIAL RATES FOR GROUPS)
LOCATION	VERY NEAR AYLESFORD
	(SEE MAP)
RULES	CHILDREN TO BE ACCOMPANIED BY AN ADULT
	NO DOGS ALLOWED
	DO NOT FEED THE ANIMALS

FURTHER INFORMATION: TELEPHONE 01394 527168

TEXT

1 What is the purpose of:

a) the map in the top right-hand corner? b) the plan of the farm?
c) the key to the plan? d) the telephone number?

2 Which town is Park Farm near?

3 On the plan of the farm what do these numbers stand for?

a) 1 b) 4 c) 7 d) 11 e) 13

4 a) What is next to the duck pond? b) How many car parks are there?
c) What runs under a bridge?

5 Explain why you think each rule is important.

SENTENCE

1 Look at the box below the plan. The information in it is not written
in proper sentences. Why do you think this is?

2 Admission Adults £2.00

When written as a proper sentence this might say:

'The price of admission for every adult is £2.00.'

Write the following as proper sentences.

a) Admission Children £1.00 b) Special rates for groups
c) Location very near Aylesford (see map) d) Children to be accompanied by an adult.
e) No dogs allowed. f) Do not feed the animals
g) Further information: Telephone 01394 527168

3 Copy this message and
underline what you think
the most important words are.

> *I will call for you at 3 o'clock. Please try and be
> ready! You will need to wear some waterproof
> shoes and a raincoat. Please bring your own
> food. We will probably be back around 7 o'clock.*

WORD

1 Copy this writing about a visit to the farm. Correct all the spelling mistakes.
Look at the leaflet or check the spellings in a dictionary if you are not sure.

We whent to Park Farm for a visite. Their were lots ov intresting fings to see.
I licked the cows and calfs and the chickins best. It was a luvly day. Wr walked
rownd the nacher trail and then had a picknick. There were swings and slids in the
play area. Mum got me an ice creem befor we left. I was verey tird wen I got home.

How to Make a Pop-up Card

What you need:
- an A4 sheet of paper
- a smaller piece of paper
- scissors
- Pritt Stick
- crayons or felt-tip pens

Step 1

Fold the sheet in half lengthways.

Step 2

Fold over the top left-hand corner. Press the corner so that it is firmly creased, then unfold it. Draw a cross on the triangle as shown.

Step 3

Unfold the sheet, keeping the cross facing you at the top.

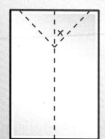

Step 4

Now fold the sheet exactly in half widthways away from you.

Step 5

Fold it again so that it is a quarter of its original size. The cross should now be on the inside of the fold.

Step 6

Pull the little triangle towards you so that it folds forward.

Step 7

On your other sheet of paper, draw a funny creature about 7 cm tall. Cut it out.

Step 8

Glue your picture firmly on to the triangle where your cross is.

Step 9

Close the card carefully so that the picture folds forwards with the triangle.

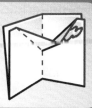

Step 10

Decorate the rest of the card with a message and pictures.

Get well soon

TEXT

1 What are the instructions on the opposite page for?

2 Why is it important to have the 'What you need' section first?

3 How many steps are there altogether?

4 Why is it helpful to have all the steps numbered and in a separate box?

5 Are the diagrams helpful? Why?

6 How clear do you think the instructions are?

7 Would it be possible to have fewer instructions? If so, how?

8 Did the diagrams help you read the instructions better? If so, how?

SENTENCE

1 Here are the instructions for running a bath. Write them out again, matching the correct endings to each instruction. Punctuate each instruction correctly.

a) put the plug	hot and cold water
b) turn on the	turn off the taps
c) put in some	a dry towel ready
d) check that the water	bubble bath
e) when the bath is nearly full	is just the right temperature
f) check that you have	the bath and have a good soak
g) get into	in the plug hole

2 Write a clear set of directions for washing your hair or making a jam sandwich.

WORD

1 There are two words from the instructions on the opposite page hiding in each line. Find them and write them down.

a) abquarterdghcreasedwq

b) trianglexzkmbvexactly

c) opjwidthwaysgoriginals

d) vcreaturehkmqwerdecorate

e) zxcvmessageaqhypcarefully

2 Write the words you found in question 1 in alphabetical order. Then write a definition for each one. Use a dictionary if you need to.

3 Use the *Look, say, cover, write, check* method to help you learn to spell the words.

The Great Flood

Long, long ago, the Great Spirit lived on the snowy summit of Takhoma. He became very angry with the people and animals of his world because they were wicked and did many bad things to each other. He decided that he would rid the earth of them all except the good animals and one good man and his family.

So he said to the good man, "Shoot an arrow into that cloud hanging low over the mountain." The good man shot an arrow and it stuck in the cloud. "Now shoot another arrow into the shaft of that arrow," continued the Great Spirit. The second arrow hit the lower part of the first arrow and stuck there. The man kept on shooting arrows and after a while there was a long rope of arrows reaching from the cloud on top of the mountain down to the ground.

"Now tell your wife and children," commanded the Great Spirit, "to climb up that rope of arrows. Tell the good animals to climb up after them. But don't let the bad people and bad animals climb up."

So the good man sent his wife up the arrow rope, then his children, then the good animals. Then the good man himself climbed up. Just as he was stepping into the cloud he looked back. Coming up the arrow rope was a long line of bad animals and snakes. So the good man broke the rope and watched them all tumble down the side of the mountain.

Then the Great Spirit caused a heavy rain to fall. It rained and rained and rained for many days and nights. All the earth was under water. The water rose higher and higher on the sides of Takhoma. At last it came up to the snow line, up to the high place where the snow leaves off in the summer time. By that time all the bad people and bad animals were drowned so the Great Spirit commanded the rain to stop. He and the good man watched the waters go slowly down. The land became dry again.

Then the Great Spirit said to the good man, "Now you may take your family and animals back to the earth." So they all climbed out of the cloud, and the good man led them down a mountain trail to the place where they were to build a new lodge. As they walked down they found no bad animals or snakes, and there have been none on Takhoma to this day.

From Indian Legends of the Pacific Northwest *by Ella Clark*

TEXT

1 Who is the most important character in this story?

2 Where does the story take place?

3 Why is the Great Spirit angry?

4 How does the Great Spirit solve the situation?

5 How does the story end?

6 What does this story tell people about the character of the Great Spirit?

7 Give the story a mark out of ten and say what you think of it.

8 Name another story that is similar to this. Explain how the two stories are similar and how they are different.

SENTENCE

1 Copy these sentences and think of a suitable word to fill each gap.

a) The Great Spirit was _____ with the _____ people.

b) The good _____ shot an _____ into a _____ .

c) The Great Spirit _____ the good man to _____ the rope of arrows.

d) When the good man looked down _____ saw some bad animals climbing the rope.

e) He broke the rope _____ watched the bad animals tumble down.

f) All the _____ flooded the earth.

g) When the water had dried _____ the man came _____ from the cloud.

h) The good man and his family lived _____ ever after.

WORD

1 Say these words. Listen to how they can be broken into two parts (syllables). Copy each word and then write it in syllables. Do it like this: became = be + came.

a) because   **b)** decide   **c)** except   **d)** hanging   **e)** forest   **f)** dentist
g) mountain   **h)** children   **i)** himself   **j)** football   **k)** slowly   **l)** under
m) lower   **n)** magnet   **o)** snowy   **p)** summer   **q)** arrow   **r)** wicked

2 Choose five of the words. Write five sentences using one of the words each time.

3 Look back at some other stories in this book. Write down ten more words with two syllables.

4 Write down five words with three syllables.

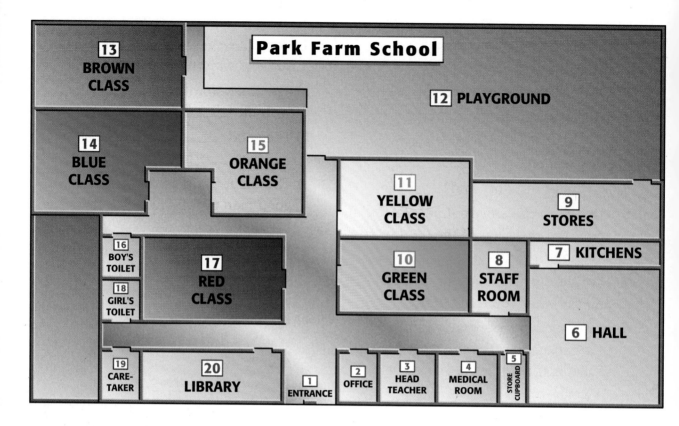

This is a plan of Park Farm School.

1 Copy this key to the plan. Finish it off in your book. ▶

2 Write the directions to the following places from the entrance doors. Look at the directions on the Notice Board on this page to help you.

    a) the hall   *b)* Yellow Class   *c)* Orange Class
    d) the stores

3 Write the directions to the following places from the Yellow Class.

    a) the kitchens   *b)* the library   *c)* Brown Class
    d) the girls' toilet

4 Choose another place to start. Make up some directions to two different places.

KEY
1. Entrance
2. Office

NOTICE BOARD

To get from the entrance to the Head Teacher's office, you come in and turn right. The office is the second on the right.

5 Imagine a new family moved next door. Their child is due to start coming to your school next week. Write some instructions you would give the child. Here are some ideas to help you get going.

> What do you need to take with you?
> How do you know when it is time to go in?
> Where do you hang your coat and bag?
> What happens when the register is called?
> What things doesn't your teacher like?
> What do you do at playtime?
> What happens at lunchtime?
> ◆ What do you do at the end of the day?

NO JUMPING ON THE BEDS

because it makes a mess!

Rule   **Reason**

6 Write down some rules you have in your school. Explain why you have them.

7 Make a poster showing a rule you have at home and the reason for it.

◆ Try it out in rough first.

◆ Make the lettering big and bold.

◆ Check the spelling.

Sentences
Do your sentences make sense?

Punctuation
Have you punctuated it correctly with capital letters, full stops, question marks, exclamation marks and commas?

Spelling
Have you checked for silly spelling mistakes?
Have you looked up any words you are not sure of?

Handwriting
Is your handwriting easy to read?

How are you getting on with the things in the chart? If you need extra practice try the activities shown.

Grammar and punctuation	Notes	1
	Writing accurate and sensible sentences	2
	General punctuation	3
Spelling phonics and vocabulary	Definitions	4
	Alphabetical order	5
	Compound words	6
	Syllables	7
	Spelling strategies	8, 9 and 10

Gone shopping – Tea on table. Do homework! Wash up!

1 Write this note again in proper sentences.

2 Copy these sentences. Correct the underlined verbs.

a) The girl <u>felled</u> off her horse.   *b)* I <u>wants</u> some toast.

c) The boy was <u>took</u> to the doctors.   *d)* I <u>gived</u> my friend some sweets.

e) The children <u>was</u> very noisy.

3 Punctuate these sentences correctly in your book.

a) what is the time

b) oh no all my spellings are wrong

c) paul the tall boy threw the ball over the wall

d) in my bag I had an apple a book and some pencils

e) sitting down slowly the old man groaned

f) it was still along way to dover the town where I lived

4 Match up the sentence beginnings and endings to make some definitions. Use the glossary at the back of this book to help you.

a) An adjective   is a naming word.

b) A noun   are words that have similar meanings.

c) A verb   is a describing word.

d) Synonyms   is often a doing word.

5 Arrange these words in alphabetical order:

a) fat, light, short, heavy, good   *b)* fast, wooden, round, old, closed

c) tame, square, gentle, fierce, clean   *d)* crisp, call, chess, clever, circle

e) seat, silly, save, shine, scent   *f)* pencil, pine, phone, pant, plan

6 Write these compound words as word sums, like this:
timetable = time + table

a) postcard   *b)* shopkeeper   *c)* bulldog   *d)* tablet

e) footstep   *f)* rabbit

7 Copy these words. Break them into syllables.
Do it like this:

> metal = met + al

a) outside   *b)* until   *c)* pocket   *d)* tablet

e) footstep   *f)* rabbit

8 Write two words for each answer. The pairs of words must contain the given phoneme, e.g.

> 'ar' – farmer, postcard

a) ar   *b)* er   *c)* ir   *d)* or   *e)* ur   *f)* aw   *g)* ew
h) ow

9 Choose 10 words you need to learn from the back cover of this book. Use the *Look, say, cover, write, check* method to help you learn them. Use the *Handy hints for spelling* to help.

10 When you can spell the words make up some sentences and use the words in them.

Handy hints for spelling

◆ Is the word spelt as it sounds? Does it contain any phonemes you already know?

◆ Does the word look right? Do you know any other words like it?

◆ Can you break the word into smaller parts? Which is the most difficult part of the word?

◆ Do you know what the word means?

◆ Have you used a word book or dictionary to help you?

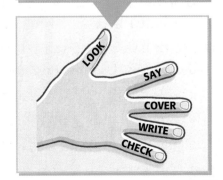

LOOK
SAY
COVER
WRITE
CHECK

On the Run

Thomas comes from a country in Africa. His father, who was Prime Minister there, is in prison in England. Thomas is staying in England and has made friends with a boy called Ben. The two boys suspect that Thomas is in danger from his uncles and Miss Fisher who look after him. Ben decides to help Thomas escape.

Ben moved cautiously towards the house. All the windows were dark; black squares in the blackness of the house wall. Ben stood at the foot of the fire-escape, looking up. Perhaps he could find Thomas' bedroom. Thomas was almost certain to be in bed by now. Miss Fisher wasn't the sort of woman to let a boy stay up late. If he could find Thomas' bedroom he could tell him the good news and go straight home, quick and silent as a thief in the night...

But as he climbed the first flight of rusty iron stairs, Ben's heart was pounding. Suppose Miss Fisher were to catch him – or one of the uncles. The terrible Uncle Tuku in his chief's robes! Ben thought about Uncle Tuku and moved more slowly; with each step he took his feet seemed to grow heavier until it was like heaving two balls of lead. Once he kicked a little stone that had somehow got onto the fire-escape and it rattled down and down, with a dreadful, ear-splitting, heart-stopping sound. Ben stood still, half expecting all the windows in the house to blaze suddenly with light. None of them did.

On the first floor, the lower half of a window was open. He peered in. It was dark inside and the drawn curtains were heavy and thick, moving only very little in the light breeze. For a moment he waited, shivering, although the night was warm. Then he thought of Thomas, lying awake in the dark and worrying about his father, and pulled himself up, over the window-sill.

As his feet touched the floor inside the room, the light was switched on.

He stood, so rigid with fright that for a moment or two, though he heard voices, he had no idea what they were saying. He just closed his eyes and waited – waited for the curtains to be torn open, for the certain discovery. But...

Nina Bawden

TEXT

1 *a)* What was Ben trying to do?   *b)* Why was he doing this?

2 From the clues in the passage, describe what you know about the house.

3 What did Ben think of: *a)* Miss Fisher   *b)* Uncle Tuku?

4 How can you tell Ben and Thomas were good friends?

5 Copy and complete this sentence: A good friend is someone who…

6 Name two things that made Ben frightened.

7 The author makes the story seem very frightening.
Write down some of the words, phrases and sentences that she used to do this.

8 Write some sentences to show how you think the story continues.

SENTENCE

1 Copy these sentences. Fill in the gaps with the adjectives used in the story.
   a) Ben climbed the _____ fire-escape.   *b)* The curtains were _____ .
   c) There was a _____ breeze.   *d)* The night was _____ .

2 Fill in each gap with an adjective which makes the noun sound frightening.
   a) a _____ window   *b)* a _____ night   *c)* a _____ noise
   d) a _____ wind   *e)* a _____ shadow   *f)* some _____ cries

3 Copy and complete these wheels with suitable adjectives like the first one.

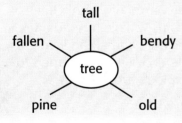

WORD

1 Choose either the prefix 'mis' or 'ex' to begin each word:
   a) take   *b)* tend   *c)* port   *d)* place   *e)* plode

2 Choose five of the words above. Write sentences using those words,
to show you know their meaning.

3 *a)* Use a dictionary. Find three words beginning with these prefixes:
   'anti' e.g. anticlockwise   'non' e.g. non-slip
   b) Write the meaning of each word.

4 Write and say what you have discovered about the prefixes 'anti' and 'non'.

Fantastic Mr Fox

The three farmers are angry with Mr Fox because he steals from them to feed his family. They decide to hide outside his fox hole and shoot him when he comes out.

"Don't get careless," said Mrs Fox. "You know they'll be waiting for you, all three of them."

"Don't worry about me," said Mr Fox. "I'll see you later."

But Mr Fox would not have been quite so cocky had he known exactly where the three farmers were waiting at that moment. They were just outside the entrance to the hole, each one crouching behind a tree with his gun loaded. And what is more, they had chosen their positions very carefully, making sure that the wind was not blowing from them towards the fox's hole. In fact, it was blowing in the opposite direction. There was no chance of them being 'smelled out'.

Mr Fox crept up the dark tunnel to the mouth of his hole. He poked his long handsome face out into the night air and sniffed once.

He moved an inch or two forward and stopped. He sniffed again. He was always especially careful when coming out of his hole.

He inched forward a little more. The front half of his body was now in the open.

His black nose twitched from side to side, sniffing and sniffing for the scent of danger. He found none, and he was just about to go trotting forward into the wood when he heard, or thought he heard a tiny noise, a soft rustling sound, as though someone had moved a foot ever so gently through a patch of dry leaves.

Mr Fox flattened his body against the ground and lay very still, his ears pricked. He waited a long time, but he heard nothing more.

"It must have been a field-mouse," he told himself, "or some other small animal."

He crept a little further out of the hole...then further still. He was almost right out in the open now. He took a last careful look around. The wood was murky and very still. Somewhere in the sky the moon was shining.

Just then, his sharp night-eyes caught a glint of something bright behind a tree not far away. It was a small silver speck of moonlight shining on a polished surface. Mr Fox lay still, watching it. What on earth was it? Now it was moving. It was coming up and up.... Great heavens! It was the barrel of a gun! Quick as a whip, Mr Fox jumped back in his hole and at the same time the entire wood seemed to explode around him.

Roald Dahl

T E X T

1 Describe how Mr Fox comes out of his hole. Make a note of each step he took, like this:

Step 1: Mr Fox poked his nose out of his hole and sniffed once.

Step 2: Then he…

2 Underline any words in the sentences you wrote in question 1 that give you a clue about the order or the time, e.g. first, then.

3 How did the farmers make sure Mr Fox would not know they were there?

4 What 'gave away' the farmers?

5 Explain what these phrases mean.

a) smelled out   *b)* scent of danger   *c)* his ears pricked

6 Some points in the story could be true. Copy the things that could be true.

Foxes steal rabbits.   Foxes live in holes.   Farmers don't like foxes.   Foxes talk to each other.   Foxes have a good sense of smell.   Foxes know what a gun is.

7 Who do you feel most sorry for – the farmers or the foxes? Say why.

S E N T E N C E

1 Write down who or what each pronoun stands for in these sentences.
Do it like this:
"They (the farmers) will be waiting for you (Mr Fox)," she (Mrs Fox) said.

a) "I ( ) am going now," Mr Fox said.   *b)* She ( ) told Mr Fox to be careful.
c) Mr Fox told her ( ) not to worry.   *d)* He ( ) moved slowly out of the hole.

2 Copy these pronouns and write whether each one is singular (S) or plural (P).

a) I (S)   *b)* me   *c)* he   *d)* him   *e)* she   *f)* her   *g)* it   *h)* we

3 Say whether the pronoun 'you' is singular or plural in these sentences.

a) "I want you to listen carefully," the teacher said to the children.
b) "Can you come out?" Emma asked Tom.

W O R D

1 Join each word in Set A to a word from Set B to make a compound word.

Do it like this: moon + light = moonlight

Set A wind snow hand air run butter black foot wheel play

Set B ground bag way mill chair man port ball cup bird

2 Use the *Look, say, cover, write, check* method to help you learn to spell the words.

3 Write some sentences and use the compound words from question 1 in them.

Sophie Meets the BFG

The Giant picked up the trembling Sophie with one hand and carried her across the cave and put her on the table. Now he really is going to eat me, Sophie thought.

The Giant sat down and stared hard at Sophie. He had truly enormous ears. Each one was as big as the wheel of a truck and he seemed to be able to move them onwards and outwards from his head as he wished.

"I is hungry!" the Giant boomed. He grinned, showing massive square teeth. The teeth were very white and square and they sat in his mouth like huge slices of white bread.

"P...Please don't eat me," Sophie stammered.

The Giant let out a bellow of laughter.

"Just because I is a Giant, you think I is a man-gobbling cannybull!" he shouted. "You is about right! Giants is all cannybully and murderful! And they does eat up human beans! We is in Giant Country now! Giants is everywhere around! Out there us has the famous Bonecrunching Giant! Bonecrunching Giant crunches up two wopsey whiffling human beans for supper every night! Noise is earbursting! Noise of crunching bones goes crackety-crack for miles around!"

"Ouch!" said Sophie.

"Bonecrunching Giant only gobbles human beans from Turkey," the Giant said. "Every night Bonecruncher is galloping off to Turkey to gobble Turks."

Sophie's sense of patriotism was so bruised by this remark that she became quite angry. "Why Turks?" she blurted out. "What's wrong with the English?"

"Bonecrunching Giant says Turks is tasting oh ever so much juicier and more scrumdiddlyumptious! Bonecruncher says Turkish human beans has a glamourly flavour. He says Turks from Turkey is tasting of turkey."

From The BFG *by Roald Dahl*

Roald Dahl is one of the most popular children's authors in the world. Roald didn't much enjoy school himself, and found teachers too strict. Before taking up writing, Roald led an adventurous life, spending time in Africa, tangling with animals and crashing a plane during the war. When Roald found he had a talent for writing he never looked back. Roald had a sense of humour that appeals to children and loved being rude. *Charlie and the Chocolate Factory* is one of the best-selling books of all time. Other favourites include *The BFG, Revolting Rhymes* and *Fantastic Mr Fox*.

TEXT

1 How can you tell that Sophie was frightened of the giant at first?

2 Find clues that tell you the giant was really friendly.

3 What is unusual about the way the giant talks?

4 *a)* Which story do you prefer – *Fantastic Mr Fox* or this one? Say why.

b) How are the two stories different?

c) How are the stories similar?

5 *a)* Who is the author?

b) Write something interesting that you discovered about him.

c) Name some other books he has written.

6 Name another author you like. Write some information on him or her. (Look on book covers, in encyclopaedias etc.)

SENTENCE

1 Copy these sentences and correct the verbs in them.

a) She are a girl.

b) The giant pick her up.

c) He were friendly.

d) She like the giant.

e) I is hungry.

f) You is right.

g) We is in Giant Country.

h) They is everywhere.

2 Now circle the pronoun in each sentence you have written.

3 The BFG uses suffixes incorrectly, e.g. murderful, glamourly. Invent some nonsense words of your own, ending with the suffixes 'ful' and 'ly'.

4 Collect some of your favourite 'giant' words. Make up some more sentences that the giant might say.

WORD

1 The giant was tall (huge, enormous, gigantic). The words in brackets are synonyms. Use a thesaurus and write down some synonyms for: *a)* loud *b)* shout *c)* eat *d)* grin

2 Use a dictionary. Write a definition for each word below to show you know the difference in meaning between these pairs of homonyms:

a) allowed, aloud *b)* dear, deer *c)* fir, fur *d)* groan, grown
e) meat, meet *f)* threw, through

3 Write some sentences to show you know how to use these homonyms.

Treasure Island

This is the famous story told by young Jim Hawkins of how he finds a treasure map belonging to the notorious pirate, Captain Flint. Jim sets sail on the good ship Hispaniola with Squire Trelawney and Captain Smollett to find the treasure. The ship's cook, Long John Silver, plans to double-cross them.

Treasure Island looked a gloomy, forbidding place. The lower parts were wooded, with rocky peaks jutting above the trees. Even in the sunshine, with birds soaring above, I hated the thought of it. We were anchored in an inlet where trees came down to the water. The air was hot and still, and the men were restless and grumbling. Captain Smollett gave leave for the men to go ashore, which raised their spirits. I believe the silly fellows thought they would break their shins over treasure as soon as they landed. Long John Silver was in charge of the two boats taking the thirteen men ashore. I knew I should not be needed on board so I decided to go ashore too.

I ran up the beach into the woods, glad to be free and alone. I sat quietly hidden in the bushes. Hearing voices, I moved nearer to catch the words. I could see and hear Long John Silver bullying a sailor to join him and the pirates. The sailor angrily refused. Silver's answer was to plunge his dagger into the man and leave him lying dead in the forest. I felt faint and the whole world swam around me in a whirling mist. When I pulled myself together, Silver, crutch under his arm, was wiping his knife on a tuft of grass. I feared for my life if I should be found, and ran and ran, not caring where.

When I stopped I was at the foot of a stony hill. My eye was caught by a movement on the hillside. I could not tell if it was a man or an animal. Here was a new danger I felt I could not face, and I began to run towards the shore. But the creature was faster than me and, darting from tree to tree, he came closer. I could now see that it was a man, but so wild and strange that I was afraid. As he neared me he threw himself on the ground, and held up his hands as if begging for mercy. I have never seen such a ragged creature. He was dressed in patchwork of odd clothes and goat skins, and his blue eyes looked startling in a face burned black by the sun.

Adapted from the story by Robert Louis Stevenson

TEXT

1 What is the name of: **a)** the ship **b)** the captain **c)** the ship's cook?

2 a) Who is telling the story? **b)** What is his name?

3 How does the author make you think the island is not a nice place?

4 Retell the main events of the passage in five sentences, like this:

The ship reached Treasure Island. Long John Silver took some men ashore.

5 Describe Jim's feelings when:

a) he saw the island **b)** he saw a sailor killed **c)** he met the strange man

6 a) Describe the strange man. **b)** Who do you think he is?

c) Write some sentences to say what you think happens next

SENTENCE

1 The story is written in the 'first' person. It seems as if it is written by Jim.

Rewrite paragraph 2 in the 'third' person, as if it was written about Jim.

Do it like this: Jim ran up the beach into the woods.

2 Choose three more sentences from the story and write them in the third person.

3 These sentences are written in the third person.

Mr Fox crept up the dark tunnel to the mouth of his hole. He moved an inch or two forward and stopped. He sniffed again. He was always especially careful when coming out of his hole.

Write them again in the first person, like this: I crept up the dark tunnel to...

WORD

1 Copy these ten tricky words from the story.

famous   treasure   double   anchor   quietly
creature   pirate   thought   catch   answer

◆ Look carefully at each word.   ◆ Underline the tricky part of each word.
◆ Write each word again. No copying!   ◆ Check your spellings.
◆ Any mistakes? Try them again!

2 You can make up sentences about tricky words to help you remember them, like this: An island is land surrounded by water. Make up some sentences about these words. (They can be as silly as you like!)

a) hear   **b)** piece   **c)** captain   **d)** balloon
e) sandwich **f)** sword   **g)** breakfast **h)** cupboard

Face to Face with a Tiger

This article comes from a magazine called It happened to me! *in which readers write in with extraordinary things that have happened to them. In it, Tony Russell describes how he will never forget the tiger he met in Nepal.*

Last year I went to Nepal for three months to work in a hospital. I think it's important to see as much of the country as you can, but it is difficult to travel around Nepal. The hospital let me have a few days' holiday, so I decided to go into the jungle and I asked a Nepalese guide, Kamal Rai, to go with me.

We started preparing for the trip at six in the morning, and left camp with two elephants carrying our equipment. It was hot, but Kamal made me wear shoes and trousers to protect me from snakes. In the jungle there was a lot of wildlife, but we were trying to find big cats, especially tigers.

We climbed onto the elephants' backs to get a better view, but it is unusual to find tigers in the afternoon because they sleep in the heat of the day. Then, in the distance, we saw a tiger, and Kamal told me to be very quiet. We crept a little nearer and found a dead deer, still bleeding. This was the tiger's lunch! Suddenly I started to feel very frightened.

We heard the tiger a second before we saw it. It jumped out like a flash of lightning, over five hundred kilos in weight and four metres long. I looked into its eyes and face, and saw right down the animal's throat. It grabbed Kamal's leg between its teeth, but I managed to pull Kamal away. One of our elephants ran at the tiger and made it go back into the grass, so we quickly escaped to let the tiger eat its lunch. That night it was impossible to sleep!

TEXT

1 Who wrote the magazine article?

2 Is it true (fact) or made-up (fiction)? Explain how you know.

3 How do you think Tony felt as he and Kamal prepared for the trip?

4 List some of the things they might have taken with them on the trip.

5 Do you think they were brave or foolish to approach the dead deer? Why?

6 Why did Tony suddenly begin to feel frightened?

7 Was Tony brave or foolish to stay and help his friend? Give a reason.

8 Why do you think Tony found it impossible to sleep that night?

9 Rewrite the main events again in the third person, like this:
Last year Tony Russell went to Nepal. He went into the jungle...

SENTENCE

1 Change the order of the words in these sentences so they make more sense.
a) For three months in a hospital Tony went to work.
b) Into the jungle Tony decided to go.
c) He chose a guide to go with him, Kamal Rai.
d) We left with our equipment, carrying two elephants.

2 Rewrite these pairs of sentences. Use a suitable conjunction to join them and make them into one sentence, e.g. It was raining. I took my umbrella. It was raining so I took my umbrella.
a) It was raining. I took my umbrella.   *b)* I went home. I had my tea.
c) Tom got wet. It was raining.   *d)* My car is red. Sam's car is blue.
e) I worked hard. The teacher was in the room.
f) Sam got her sums wrong. She didn't know how to do them.

WORD

1 Break these words into syllables like this: pro + tect = protect
a) because   *b)* nearer   *c)* between   *d)* quickly   *e)* bleeding   *f)* distance

2 Write down these words and say if they have two or three syllables.
Do it like this: hospital (3), because (2).
a) jungle   *b)* country   *c)* important   *d)* hospital   *e)* started   *f)* difficult

3 Read *Treasure Island* again (Unit 3.4). Find five two-syllable words and five three-syllable words in it.

What comes next?

Use Unit 3.1 to help you write your own story. Read the passage again. Imagine you are Ben. Copy this sentence and continue the story.

> I had just climbed through the dark window when suddenly a bright light was switched on …

Story plans

1 Here are the bones of a story about *Treasure Island*. They are in the wrong order. Write them again in a better order.

2 Write the bones of the story in Unit 3.5 in the same way.

Story sequel

Read Unit 3.2 again. Fantastic Mr Fox is always getting the better of the three farmers. Write another story in which he outsmarts them again.

You sail home with the treasure.

Some of the crew plan to steal the treasure.

You find an old treasure map.

You have some problems on the island.

You hire a ship and sail to Treasure Island.

You search for the treasure.

Write your own story

Choose one of the story plans. Use it to help you write your own story. Use the *Handy hints for writing stories* to help you.

EXTRA IDEA

Why not make your story into a book?
Give each separate part of your story a chapter heading.
Start it on a separate piece of paper.
Number your pages and make a contents page.
Design a front and
back cover for your book.
Don't forget the illustrations!
Write some
information about
the author on the
back cover.

Book reviews

Choose a unit from Units 3.1–3.4.

Use the *Book review checklist* to help you write a review of it.

Book review checklist

What was the title of the book and who was the author?
Who was the main character (or characters)?
Who was your favourite character? Why?
Was there a character you did not like? Why?
Where did the story take place?
What was your favourite part of the story?
Did you like the way the author wrote the story?
Would you recommend the story to a friend? Say why.

Handy hints for writing stories

Setting

◆ Where will your story take place?

◆ When will it take place – in the past? now? in the future?

Characters

◆ Who will be in your story – people you know? made-up people? animals?

◆ What will they look like?

◆ What sort of things will they do?

Plot

◆ What will your story be about?

◆ How will it begin?

◆ What sort of things will happen in the middle?

◆ How will the story end – will it be sad or happy? exciting or mysterious?

> How are you getting on with the things in the chart? If you need extra practice try the activities shown.

Grammar and punctuation	Adjectives	1
	Pronouns	2
	Writing accurate and sensible sentences	3 and 4
	Writing in the 1st and 3rd person	5
Spelling phonics and vocabulary	Synonyms and homonyms	6 and 7
	Compound words	8
	Prefixes	9
	Syllables	10
	Spelling strategies	11,12 and 13

1 Copy and complete these sentences with suitable adjectives.

One _____ night Hansel and Gretel went for a _____ walk and got lost in a _____ forest. They came across an _____ house and saw a _____ light coming from a _____ window. A _____ lady came out. She looked very_____ . "We are lost," said Hansel in a _____ voice. "Can you help us?"

2 Circle all the pronouns in the sentences you wrote for (1).

3 Rewrite these sentences so they make more sense.

a) The computer typed a letter on the secretary.

b) The bone woke up and ate the dog.

c) The egg boiled the man in the saucepan.

d) Her teddy bear a girl hugged.

4 Copy these sentences. Fill in the gaps with 'was' or 'were' so they make sense.

Nazreen _____ climbing a tree. She _____ near the top. Suddenly there _____ a cry. Her foot slipped. She _____ falling! Luckily her mum and dad _____ under the tree and caught her. "You _____ lucky we _____ here," they said.

5 Question 4 is written in the 3rd person. Rewrite it in the 1st person as if you are telling the story. Do it like this: I was climbing a tree.

6 Use a thesaurus or dictionary. Write a synonym that means the same as:

a) walk *b)* thief *c)* centre *d)* hunt *e)* collect
f) terrible

7 Write sentences to show you know the difference between these homonyms:

a) sea/see *b)* roar/raw *c)* weight/wait
d) night/knight

8 Add the words from Set B to the words in Set A to make compound words, e.g.
wild + life = wildlife

SET A	wild	news	rail	day	wheel	wind	under
SET B	screen	life	way	ground	barrow	light	paper

9 Take the prefixes off these words. Write the words you are left with.
a) mistreat *b)* express *c)* cooperate *d)* anticlimax
e) nonsense

10 Copy the words below. Say if they have 2 or 3 syllables, like this:

> *hun ter = 2 syllables*

a) window *b)* horrible *c)* September *d)* except
e) lemon *f)* determine *g)* promise *h)* perfectly
i) limit *j)* together

11 Write four words containing each letter string:
'ie', 'aw', 'ough', 'age', 'tch'.

12 Choose 10 words you need to learn from the back cover of this book. Use the *Look, say, cover, write, check* method to help you learn them. Use the *Handy hints for spelling* to help.

Handy hints for spelling

◆ Is the word spelt as it sounds? Does it contain any phonemes you already know?

◆ Does the word look right? Do you know any other words like it?

◆ Can you break the word into smaller parts? Which is the most difficult part of the word?

◆ Do you know what the word means?

◆ Have you used a word book or dictionary to help you?

Poems for Fun

The Adventures of Isabel

Isabel met an enormous bear,
Isabel, Isabel, didn't care;
The bear was hungry, the bear was ravenous,
The bear's big mouth was cruel and cavernous.
The bear said, "Isabel, pleased to meet you.
How do, Isabel, now I'll eat you!"
Isabel, Isabel, didn't worry,
Isabel didn't scream or scurry,
She washed her hands and she straightened her hair up,
Then Isabel quietly ate the bear up!

Ogden Nash

The Flea and the Fly

A fly and a flea in a flue
Were wondering what they should do.
Said the fly, "Let us flee!"
Said the flea, "Let us fly!"
So they flew through a flaw in the flue!

The Tale of the Poor Peanut

A peanut sat on the railway track
Its heart was all a-flutter.
Along came a train, the 10.15 –
Toot! Toot! – peanut butter!

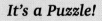

It's a Puzzle!

Where can a man buy a cap for his knee
Or a key for the lock of his hair?
And can the eyes be called a school?
I should think so – there are some pupils there!

TEXT

1 Which poems made you smile?

2 Which poem made you think hard?

3 Which poem was a tongue twister?

4 Which poem did you enjoy best? Give your reasons.

5 *a)* How would you describe Isabel?
b) How would you describe the bear?

6 Find and write down the word that rhymes with 'a-flutter'.

7 What do these pairs of words mean? Look them up in a dictionary.

   a) flea and flee   *b)* flew and flue

8 Where would you find each of these things in your body? Where else would you find each thing? e.g. My nose has a bridge and so does a river.

   a) crown   *b)* roof   *c)* crook
   d) drum   *e)* calf   *f)* palm

SENTENCE

Here is another verse about Isabel but some of the words do not make sense. Write the verse again and correct the words with lines through.

*Isabel once ~~were~~ asleep in bed
When a horrible dream ~~crawl~~ into her head.
It was ~~worser~~ than a dinosaur, worse than a shark,
Worse than ~~a~~ octopus in the dark.
 "Boo!" ~~say~~ the dream, with a dreadful ~~grins~~,
"I ~~is~~ going to scare you right out of ~~her~~ skin!"
Isabel, Isabel, didn't worry,
Isabel didn't ~~screamed~~ or scurry,
Isabel ~~have~~ a clever scheme;
She just ~~woked~~ up and fooled that dream.*

WORD

1 Make some new words, like this:

   a) Change the b in bear to p, t, w.
   b) Change the p in pair to f, h, l, st.
   c) Change the c in care to d, f, r, sh, st, squ.
   d) Change the s in saw to cl, fl, j, l, p, r.
   e) Change the m in more to b, c, ch, sh, t, w.

2 Write down as many words as you can that contain these letter patterns.

   a) 'ear' as in near   *b)* 'ird' as in bird   *c)* 'ar' as in car   *d)* 'ow' as in cow

Writing Letters

Last week the Khan family each wrote a letter.

12 Ryman Avenue
Bedford
BD2 6TS

December 4th
1998

Dear Mrs James

Shireen has to go to the dentist on Thursday at 2 o'clock. Would it be possible for me to pick her up after lunch?

Yours sincerely

Reza Khan

Mr Reza Khan

---

12 Ryman Avenue
Bedford
BD2 6TS
December 4th 1998

Dear Sirs

I recently bought one of your new Super Jet vacuum cleaners. I am not at all happy with it. One of the wheels was broken and it does not seem to suck up crumbs or dust very well. I am most disappointed. I really think you should do something about it urgently.

I would welcome an early reply to my letter.

Yours faithfully

S. Khan

Mrs S. Khan

---

12 Ryman Avenue
Bedford
BD2 6TS
December 4th 1998

Dear Gran,

Thank you for the money you sent me for my birthday. For months I have wanted a pair of pink trainers and now I will have enough money to get them. They will make me run even faster! I hope we can come and see you soon, then I can show you my trainers.

Love

Shireen

TEXT

1 What does each letter have in the top right-hand corner?

2 Write your name and full address (including postcode) on an envelope.

3 Who is each person writing to?

4 Which letter is:

   a) a thank-you letter
   b) a complaint
   c) a request?

5 How do you know who each letter is from?

6 Which is the friendliest letter? Give your reasons.

7 Which letter is the least friendly? Give your reasons.

8 Is Mrs Khan's letter polite or rude?

9 a) Why has Mr Khan signed his letter 'Yours sincerely'?

   b) Why has Mrs Khan signed her letter 'Yours faithfully'?

SENTENCE

1 Copy the sentences. Underline the possessive pronoun in each sentence.

   a) Here comes my Mum.
   b) Can I borrow your pencil?
   c) The boy lost his bag.
   d) The girl found her pen.
   e) The dog wagged its tail.
   f) We love our school.
   g) The children listened to their teacher.

2 Copy the sentences. Fill in the missing possessive pronouns correctly.

   a) This is my book. It is _____.
   b) Is this your cat? Is it_____?
   c) This car belongs to her. It is_____.
   d) Washing up is their job. The job is _____.

WORD

1 Copy these questions and write down suitable answers.

   a) *You:* Hi, Emma. How's it going?
   Emma:

   b) *You:* Hello, Mrs Shahani. How are you?
   Mrs Shahani:

   c) *You:* Open that door, please.
   Emma:

   d) *You:* Please open the door for me.
   Stranger:

2 Copy these answers and write down suitable questions.

   a) *Mum:*   *You:* Yes, please.

   b) *You:*   *Visitor:* Thank you. That is very kind.

3 Write down how you would tell these people they are in your seat.

   a) a friend   b) a stranger

4 Write down all the ways you can think of to:

   a) greet someone   b) say goodbye   c) express surprise

Information Books

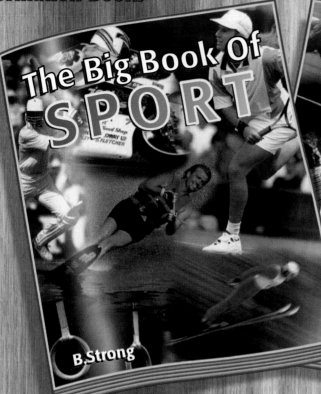

The Big Book Of SPORT

B.Strong

Do you want to know how to
• play tennis?
• head a football?
• run faster?
• throw a javelin?
• or learn many other sports?
Ben Strong, the famous sports personality, teaches you all you need to know in easy steps

Contents page

Index

TEXT

1 *a)* What is the title of the book?   *b)* Who is B. Strong?

2 *a)* What is the purpose of a contents page?   *b)* Where would you find it?

3 Name three sports you might find in the 'Ball games' section of the book.

4 *a)* What is the purpose of an index?   *b)* Where would you find it?
c) Copy and complete: The sports in the index are in _____ order.

5 On which page would you find the following sports?
a) boxing   *b)* football   *c)* ice skating   *d)* netball   *e)* swimming

6 Copy the names of these sports. Tick them if they are in the book.
Cross them if they are not.
a) basketball   *b)* cricket   *c)* rounders   *d)* hockey   *e)* golf
f) discus   *g)* snooker   *h)* judo   *i)* wrestling   *j)* baseball

7 List some types of books that are set out in alphabetical order, e.g. a dictionary.

8 Choose four sports. Write a paragraph about each. Give each paragraph its
own heading. Arrange the paragraphs in alphabetical order.

SENTENCE

1 Write these sentences as if they happened yesterday. Change the verbs.
Do it like this: I kick a ball. Yesterday I kicked a ball.
a) I throw a javelin.   *b)* I run a race.   *c)* I hop, skip and jump.   *d)* I hit the ball.
e) I swim in a race.   *f)* I get wet.   *g)* I ride my bike.   *h)* I fall over.

2 Copy the sentences. Underline the conjunction in each.
a) I went home because it was late.   *b)* I felt ill so I called a doctor.
c) I kept trying until I scored a goal.   *d)* I went indoors when it rained.

WORD

1 Copy these words and put in the missing apostrophes:
a) Im   *b)* youre   *c)* hes   *d)* shes   *e)* its   *f)* were
g) theyre   *h)* dont   *i)* cant   *j)* wouldnt   *k)* couldnt   *l)* hasnt

2 Write three sports which end with 'ball'.

3 Write the sports which end with the suffix 'ing'.

4 Which sport has   *a)* the most letters   *b)* the fewest letters?

5 Choose five sports that are hard to spell. Underline the tricky bits in each.
Use the *Look, say, cover, write, check* method to learn them.

Playing with Words

Knock! Knock!
Who's there?
Cornflakes.
Cornflakes who?
I'll tell you next week.
It's a cereal!

Knock! Knock!
Who's there?
Frank.
Frank who?
Frank you very much!

Knock! Knock!
Who's there?
Howard.
Howard who?
Howard I know?

Can you answer these riddles?

1 What gets bigger without getting heavier?

2 What doesn't ask questions but often gets answered?

3 What is red and goes up and down?

4 A cunning-purrer,
A night-creeper,
A mouse-pouncer,
A paw-padder,
A house-minder,
A four-foot-lander.
What am I?

5 What do you kiss with?

6 What is a robin?

Read the notices and remember – punctuation matters!

PRIVATE.
No swimming allowed.

PRIVATE?
No. Swimming allowed.

Answers 1. A hole 2. A door 3. A tomato in a lift 4. A cat 5. Tulips 6. A bird that steals

TEXT

1 Write out these riddles. Match the riddles to their answers.

What kind of dog has no tail?	Rain.
What has teeth but can't bite?	A zebra on skates.
What falls but never gets hurt?	A hot dog.
What tree do you find in every house?	A giraffe with a loudspeaker.
What is black and white with eight wheels?	A lavatory (lav-a-tree).
What is tall and has a loud voice?	A comb.

2 Make up some riddles of your own for: *a)* a clock   *b)* a chair   *c)* a mirror

3 Explain what you think a riddle is.

4 Collect and write a few 'Knock! Knock!' jokes.

SENTENCE

1 Copy and punctuate this nonsense rhyme correctly.

I knew a man who always wore a saucepan on his head
I asked him what he did it for I don't know why he said
it always makes my ears so sore I am a foolish man
I should have left it off before and worn a frying pan

2 Copy and punctuate these 'Doctor' jokes.

a) Patient: doctor doctor I think I'm turning into a dustbin
   Doctor: don't talk rubbish
b) Patient: doctor doctor I'm turning invisible
   Doctor: who said that

WORD

1 There are ten words from the page opposite hiding in this puzzle.

Find them and write them in your book.

a) a b c q u e s t i o n s d e r i d d l e s h
b) c u n n i n g h j r o b i n k m n o q p
c) q r s p o u n c e r v w x k n o c k z u w
d) v a l l o w e d a r s w i m m i n g f d
e) l k j h n o t i c e m n b v a n s w e r e d

2 Underline the tricky part of each word. Learn to spell the words. Use the *Look, say, cover, write, check* method to help you learn to spell the words.

3 Write some sentences using the words from question 1 in them.

In the Library

Fiction books are usually arranged alphabetically, according to the authors' surnames.

Dewey No	Subject	Examples
000 – 099	General Reference	encylopaedias, dictionaries, etc
100 – 199	Philosophy	ideas about life
200 – 299	Religion	world religions, religious leaders
300 – 399	Social science	hospitals, post office, police, etc
400 – 499	Language	English and foreign language
500 – 599	Science	maths, chemistry, animals, etc
600 – 699	Technology	farming, building, computers
700 – 799	The Arts	music, art, dance, sport, etc
800 – 899	Literature	stories, poems, plays, etc
900 – 999	History, Geography Biography	people in the past atlases, countries, etc

TEXT

1 *a)* How are fiction books usually arranged in libraries?

   b) How are fiction books arranged in your school library?

2 Put these books in alphabetical order, according to author surnames:

   Spots in Space by Sheila Lavelle   *Flat Stanley* by Jeff Brown
   The Railway Children by E. Nesbit   *Ten in a Bed* by Allan Ahlberg

3 Explain what the Dewey System is.

4 How are non-fiction books organised in your school library?

5 In the Dewey System, which books are numbered between:

   a) 000–099   *b)* 200–299   *c)* 500–599   *d)* 900–999?

6 Using the Dewey System, where would you find:

   a) an encyclopaedia   *b)* a book on Jesus   *c)* how to learn French
   d) a book on farm animals   *e)* a book on football   *f)* a poetry book
   g) a book on the Romans?

SENTENCE

1 Copy these sentences, and correct them so they make sense.

   Our library are divided into two section. One part is for fiction book. The other part are for non-fiction books. We goes to the library two times a week. One time is to choosing an story book. The second times is for find out information on our projects. My favourite authors is Roald Dahl and Nina Bawden.

2 Find and write down the titles and authors of three fiction and three non-fiction books. Notice how capital letters are used in book titles.

WORD

1 Copy and correct the spelling mistakes in these sentences. Many of the words are on the opposite page. Use a dictionary to look up any other words you are not sure of.

   I like going to our libary. My favorit ficshon book is *On the Run* by Nina Bawden. I enjoy poetree books as well. I love looking at informashon books but sumtimes I have a bit of trubble finding them. The Dewey System is quit hard to understand. The sort of books I like looking at are compooter books and books about uther countys. I also like histry books.

2 Write the misspelt words in a list, in alphabetical order.

3 Use the Look, say, cover, write, check method to help you learn to spell the words.

4 Write some sentences using the words from question 2 in them.

Writing letters

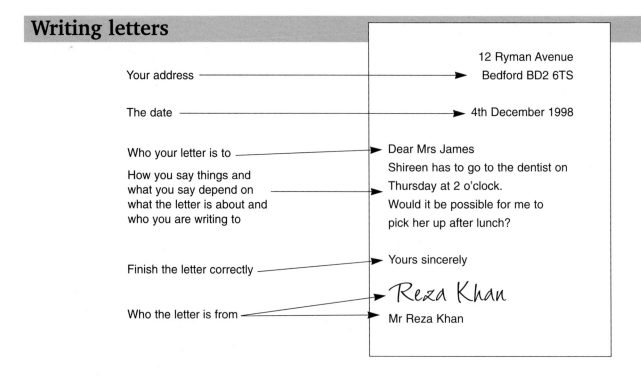

Your address ————————————————► 12 Ryman Avenue
Bedford BD2 6TS

The date ——————————————————► 4th December 1998

Who your letter is to ————————► Dear Mrs James
Shireen has to go to the dentist on
How you say things and
what you say depend on
what the letter is about and
who you are writing to

Shireen has to go to the dentist on
Thursday at 2 o'clock.
Would it be possible for me to
pick her up after lunch?

Finish the letter correctly ————► Yours sincerely

Who the letter is from ————————► *Reza Khan*
Mr Reza Khan

Choose some of these ideas for writing letters.

1 *A letter of complaint* Imagine you have just received the Treasure Island Adventure Game for your computer at school. When you open it you find that the disk is damaged and there are no instructions. Write to complain.

2 *A letter asking for information* Choose one of the characters you have read about in this book this term, e.g. the BFG. Think of three or four questions you would really like to ask the character and write to them.

3 *A letter to an author* Write and tell your favourite author how much you have enjoyed a particular book. Say what you liked about it and mention any other books by them you have read. (If you send it to the publisher of the book, they will pass your letter on to the author.)

4 *A letter of apology* Imagine you accidentally threw a ball over your fence and it broke your neighbour's window. Explain how it happened. Say sorry for the trouble and mess you have caused. Think of some things you can suggest to help make it up.

Make your own non-fiction book

- ◆ Make a book on your own or with others.
- ◆ Start each new topic on a new page.
- ◆ Give each topic a proper title.
- ◆ Illustrate your pages.
- ◆ Number your pages at the end.
- ◆ Design a cover for your book.
- ◆ Do you need a contents/index page?

An animal alphabet book

Think of one animal for each letter of the alphabet. Do some research and collect some interesting information about each animal, e.g. appearance, diet, size, where it lives etc. When you have enough information write a few sentences on each animal.

A book of favourite authors

Collect information on a number of favourite authors, e.g. name, titles of books written, type of books, personal information about author etc.

A book of sport

Make your own sports book like the one shown in Unit 3.8.

My book of favourite people

These could be characters from stories you have read, characters from history, famous sports people or entertainers etc.

Handy hints on editing your work

Sentences

Do your sentences make sense?

Punctuation

Have you punctuated it correctly with capital letters, full stops, question marks, exclamation marks and commas?

Spelling

Have you checked for silly spelling mistakes?

Have you looked up any words you are not sure of?

Handwriting

Is your handwriting easy to read?

Have you thought about doing your work on a word processor?

How are you getting on with the things in the chart? If you need extra practice try the activities shown.

Grammar and punctuation	Subject/verb agreement	1
	Ordering sentences correctly	2
	Writing accurate and sensible sentences	3
	Conjunctions	4
	General punctuation	5
Spelling phonics and vocabulary	Dictionary work	6 and 7
	Common expressions	8
	Apostrophes	9
	Spelling strategies	10, 11 and 12

1 Copy these sentences. Write the verbs as if they happened in the past. Do it like this:

Mark *takes* a bus to Jane's house.
Mark *took* a bus to Jane's house.

a) Mark and Jane *eat* quickly.

b) Mark *goes* straight to the food.

c) Jane and Mark *feel* sick.

d) The table *is* covered with lots of party food.

e) They *drink* a bottle of pop each.

2 Now write the sentences above in order so they tell a story.

3 Copy this story. Fill in the gaps with sensible words.

Ashraf was _____ a stream. _____ of the stepping stones was _____ .
His _____ slipped and _____ fell _____ the water with a _____ .
Ashraf _____ his knee. It was very _____ . His mum put _____ plaster on it
for _____ .

4 Copy these sentences and underline the conjunction in each one.

a) I went home and had my tea.

b) I can spell but I am not good at maths.

c) Tom stopped when it got dark.

d) I had some money so I spent it.

e) I will play until Mum calls.

f) I ran the race although I was tired.

5 Punctuate these sentences correctly.

  a) Can I come in tom asked
  b) do not run shouted the teacher
  c) help I am stuck cried emma
  d) I prefer tea to coffee

6 Use a dictionary. Write the definitions of these:

  a) scales   *b)* reptile   *c)* inhabit   *d)* erupt   *e)* citizen

7 Write the words above in alphabetical order.

8 Sort these common expressions into pairs according to meaning.

Hi!

Wow!

See you later

Cheerio!

How's it going?

Good morning

How are you?

9 Copy the words. Put in the apostrophes.

  a) Ive   *b)* mustnt   *c)* youll   *d)* whos   *e)* couldnt

10 Correct the spelling of these words. Use a dictionary. Write sentences containing each word.

  a) puıson   *b)* cpoer   *c)* barc   *d)* docter   *e)* peple

11 Copy and complete these sentences. Use a dictionary to check spellings.

  _ _ ce upon a time there was a wick _ _ old
  w_ _ an who l _ _ _ d in the w _ _ ds. Some
  p _ _ ple s _ _ d she was a wi _ _ _ . She lived
  in a cott _ _ _ on her _ _ n with a black cat and
  lots of t _ _ ds.

12 *a)* Choose 10 words you need to learn from the back cover of this book. Use the *Look, say, cover, write, check* method to help you learn them.

  b) Make up some sentences and use the words in them.

Handy hints for spelling

◆ Is the word spelt as it sounds? Does it contain any phonemes you already know?

◆ Does the word look right? Do you know any other words like it?

◆ Can you break the word into smaller parts? Which is the most difficult part of the word?

◆ Do you know what the word means?

◆ Have you used a word book or dictionary to help you?

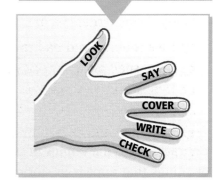

LOOK
SAY
COVER
WRITE
CHECK

Glossary

adjective

An adjective is a describing word.
It describes (adds meaning to) a noun.

a **fat** cat

alliteration

Alliteration is when we use lots of words that begin with the same sound.

Snakes **s**lide **s**lowly.

alphabetical order

Words are often put in order according to the letter or letters they begin with.

These words are in alphabetical order:

ant, bear, cat, dog

apostrophe

An apostrophe is like a raised comma.
It shows when something has
been missed out.

For example, **do not** can be written as **don't**

author

An author is someone who writes books.

characters

Characters are the names of people, animals or things that appear in stories.

chorus

A chorus is a part of a poem or song that is usually repeated after each verse.

collective noun

A collective noun is the name given to a group of persons or things, for example
a **swarm** of bees

comma

A comma is a punctuation mark. It tells you to pause.

I went home, had a sandwich and watched TV.

compound word

A compound word is when two short words are joined to make one long word.

butter + fly = **butterfly**

conjunction

A conjunction is a joining word. Conjunctions may be used to join two sentences together.

I put up my umbrella **when** it started to rain.

consonant

Letters can be divided into vowels and consonants.

The vowels are **a**, **e**, **i**, **o** and **u**. The rest of the letters of the alphabet are consonants.

contents page

A contents page appears at the beginning of a book.

It tells you the names of the sections or chapters in the book.

definition

A definition is the meaning of a word.

dialogue

A dialogue is a conversation between two people.

dictionary

A dictionary gives you the meanings of words.

Dictionaries are arranged in alphabetical order.

exclamation

An exclamation is a sentence which shows that we feel something strongly. It always ends with an exclamation mark.

Stop thief!

fact

A fact is something that is true

fable

A fable is a story with a moral. It tries to teach us something.

Animals are often used in fables.

The story of *The Hare and Tortoise* is a fable.

fiction

A fiction story is one which has not really happened. It is made up.

Non-fiction books are about things that are true.

full stop

A full stop is a dot showing that a sentence has ended. ◄——

homonym

A homonym is a word that has the same spelling as another but has a different meaning.

calf   calf

A homonym may also be a word that sounds the same as another but has a different meaning.

bear   bare

index

An index is a list at the end of a book, telling you on which pages to find particular things.

instruction

An instruction is when we tell people to do something, or teach them how to do something.

letter string

A letter string is a group of letters which occur often in words. Remembering letter patterns helps us to spell.

Here is a common letter pattern:

l**ight** br**ight** s**ight** fr**ight**

moral

A moral is a kind of lesson we can learn. It teaches us how to behave. Fables often have a moral.

narrator

A narrator is someone who tells a story.

noun

A noun is a naming word. It can be the name of a person, place or thing. (See also proper nouns and collective nouns.)

opposite

Opposites are two words whose meanings are as different as possible from each other.

hot cold

order

An order is a sort of command, when you tell someone to do something.

Pass the ball to me.

paragraph

A paragraph is a group of sentences that deals with one main idea or topic. It is easier to read a longer piece of writing if it is divided into paragraphs.

person

A piece of writing may be written in:

the **first person** – **I** said... **I** am....
the **second person** – **you** said... **you** are...
the **third person** – **he**, **she** or **it** said...
he, **she** or **it** is

phoneme

A phoneme is the smallest unit of sound in a word. It may be represented by one, two, three or four letters.

e.g. t**o** sh**oe** thr**ough**

plot

A plot is what happens in a story.

plural

Singular means one.

a book

Plural means more than one.

lots of books

poem

A poem is a piece of writing which is imaginative. It may express our thoughts or feelings. It is set out in lines. The lines may or may not rhyme.

poet

A poet is someone who writes poems.

prefix

A prefix is a group of letters we add to the beginning of words to change their meaning.

happy **un**happy

pronoun

A pronoun is a word we use instead of a noun.

This is a **personal pronoun.**

When Ben jumped in the puddle **he** got very muddy.

These are **possessive pronouns**.

These are **my** sweets. They are **mine**.

proper noun

A proper noun is the particular name of a person, place or thing. We always begin proper nouns with capital letters.

These are **proper nouns**

My name is **Sarah**. I live in **Cambridge**.

punctuation

Punctuation helps us make sense of what we read. Punctuation marks make writing easier for us to understand.

These are all punctuation marks:

Full stops | .

commas | ,

question marks | ?

exclamation marks | !

speech marks | " "

question

A question is what we ask when we want to know something. Questions always end with a **question mark**.

May I stay up and watch the late film?

rhyme

A rhyme occurs when two word have an ending that sounds the same.

h**ead** b**ed**

riddle

A riddle is a kind of puzzle to be solved by the reader.

sentence

A sentence should make sense on its own. It should begin with a **capital letter**. Most sentences end with a **full stop**.

This is a sentence.

The dog chased the postman.

This is not a sentence.
The dog

setting

A setting is where a story takes place.

silent letter

A silent letter is not pronounced when you say a word.

knee   **w**rite   com**b**

singular

(see plural)

a book

speech bubble

In comics and pictures we often write what people say inside speech bubbles.

speech marks

When we write down what someone says, we put it inside speech marks.

The giant said, "I'm hungry."

statement

A statement is a sentence that gives us information.

The dog ate a bone.

suffix

A suffix is a group of letters added to the end of a word e.g.

spider ⟶ spider**s**   cook ⟶ cook**ing**

syllable

Longer words may be broken down into smaller parts called syllables.

bad has one syllable
bad min ton has three syllables

synonym

Synonyms are words with the same, or very similar, meanings.

a **sad**, **unhappy** clown

thesaurus

A thesaurus is a book containing lists of synonyms. The words are arranged in alphabetical order.

title

A title is the name we give a book or something we have made.

verb

A verb is a doing, or being, word

The cat **scratched** my hand. The cat **was** asleep.

verse

A poem is often divided into parts, or verses.

High Frequency Word List

about	him	put	**Days of the week**	**Numbers to 20**
after	his	ran	Sunday	one
again	home	saw	Monday	two
an	house	school	Tuesday	three
another	how	seen	Wednesday	four
as	if	should	Thursday	five
back	jump	sister	Friday	six
ball	just	so	Saturday	seven
be	last	some		eight
because	laugh	take	**Months of the year**	nine
bed	little	than	January	ten
been	live(d)	that	February	eleven
boy	love	their	March	twelve
brother	made	them	April	thirteen
but	make	then	May	fourteen
by	man	there	June	fifteen
call(ed)	many	these	July	sixteen
came	may	three	August	seventeen
can't	more	time	September	eighteen
could	much	too	October	nineteen
did	must	took	November	twenty
do	name	tree	December	
don't	new	two		**Your name and address**
dig	next	us		
door	night	very	**Common colour words**	**The name and address of your school**
down	not	want	black	
first	now	water	white	
from	off	way	blue	
girl	old	were	red	
good	once	what	green	
got	one	when	yellow	
had	or	where	pink	
half	our	who	purple	
has	out	will	orange	
have	over	with	brown	
help	people	would		
her	push	your		
here	pull			